THE NO SPEND YEAR

LITTLE WAYS TO SAVE A LOT OF MONEY

Michelle McGagh

CORONET

First published in Great Britain in 2017 by Coronet
An Imprint of Hodder & Stoughton
An Hachette UK company

This paperback edition published in 2018

1

A CIP catalogue record for this title is available from the British Library

Paperback ISBN 9781473652156
eBook ISBN 9781473652132

Typeset in Garamond MT Std by Palimpsest Book Production Ltd,
Falkirk, Stirlingshire

Printed and bound Clays Ltd, St Ives plc

Hodder & Stoughton policy is to use papers that are natural, renewable
and recyclable products and made from wood grown in sustainable forests.
The logging and manufacturing processes are expected to conform to the
environmental regulations of the country of origin.

CONTENTS

THE
NO
SPEND
YEAR

INTRODUCTION

'You're not buying anything? At all? For a whole year?'

This is the phrase that I've heard a million times, usually followed by: 'I could never do that!'

And it's true, most people don't want to give up spending and treating themselves for an entire year. Most people are sensible. But lots of people do want to cut back, have more pennies in their pocket and make better financial decisions.

They just don't know where to start.

So let me start at the beginning.

The decision to set myself the challenge of a no spend year didn't happen overnight. It was the next, somewhat dramatic step in a process of taking back control of my money and my life.

In September 2013, me and my husband Frank sold our house and moved twenty doors down the road to a bigger house. We didn't really need to move and we certainly didn't need a bigger house.

But we're British, and we were swept away by that peculiarly British phenomenon of climbing the property ladder. We thought that the size of our house was a way of showing how successful we were. That was the first mistake.

The second mistake was the house was more than a doer-upper – it was almost uninhabitable, but we couldn't afford to move out so we decided to live in it, with a constant team of workmen trudging in and out.

Everything needed replacing, from the electrics to the plumbing, and every wall had to be stripped of plaster. Not content with that, we decided to also extend upwards and outwards, making a too-large home larger still.

As far as we were concerned, we were living the dream. For a short while at least.

But here's the rub when it comes to living in an uninhabitable home: it's not fun. In fact it's dirty, stressful and chaotic.

However, I should be grateful for all the dirt and stress and chaos, because it made me realise something very important: I needed far less stuff than I had.

I'd managed to accumulate an embarrassing number of things over the years, but the vast majority of it became pretty much useless to me, apart from the vacuum cleaner, as I was living on a building site.

Thanks to the renovation work, all of the things I had so diligently collected over the years had to be put into storage. Now and again over the course of the house renovation, we'd make a trip to the storage unit and be confronted by a hoard of furniture, posters, lampshades and boxes. One box in particular stands out in my mind. It was marked 'not needed', begging the question – then why did we still have it?

This toing and froing to the storage unit went on for more than six months and it began to play on my mind more and more, until one day I Googled the rather random phrase: 'get rid of stuff'. It was a daft phrase to Google, as if I needed to be told how to put things in the bin. But I'm glad I did it as it opened my eyes to a whole new world where spending and consuming were no longer King.

It was at this point I discovered minimalism and fell down a wormhole of minimalism websites, typically based in the US, where people described how they freed themselves from the tyranny of their possessions by getting rid of their stuff. They spoke of feeling lighter and of how having fewer things had benefited their lives.

Surely I couldn't do that? Get rid of all the things I owned? All the items that I believed made me cleverer and more interesting, all of the things that I used as a comfort blanket, all of the things that I had bought to create the illusion of a lifestyle I wasn't actually living.

And then something clicked.

We didn't need all of this stuff. We'd lived for six months out of two drawers each and we'd survived. Very rarely did we *need* something from the storage unit.

I discovered that minimalism wasn't about living out of a rucksack or living in an empty box of white walls; it wasn't a competition to see who could own the fewest items – it was about owning items that were either practical or that brought you pleasure.

Imagine enjoying every item you owned. Imagine not feeling burdened by the items you've kept just because someone gave them to you and you would feel guilty for throwing them away. Deciding that you're not going to beat yourself up because you no longer fit into clothes you wore ten years ago, and getting rid of them instead, along with the guilt that goes with them.

I realised that the things I owned had started to own me and I had bought things to tell people a story about who I was, or at least who I wanted them to think I was. By getting rid of those items I was taking back control of who I *really* was.

As a millennial I'd grown up being sold to through magazines and TV and I was hooked. I was happy to be told what item to buy to make me look prettier or seem cleverer or more interesting. Except none of the items ever really did what they said they would, so I did what advertising is supposed to make us do: I continued to shop on the off-chance that I would find the elusive products that I thought would make my life better.

By getting rid of the items I owned, I was finally telling the advertisers that I was on to their game, that I didn't need an object to make me happier.

I set out to try to determine what would make me genuinely happy. The starting point was to get rid of the stuff that had been crowding my house and my mind.

Luckily, Frank had been feeling the pressure of the stuff too, so we decided to get rid of as much of it as we could. Nothing was safe from being donated, given away or sold.

Crates of vintage dresses ended up on eBay; the local charity shop became the recipient of multiple 1950s and 1960s crockery sets; family benefited from rugs, chairs, lamps and pictures.

In total, after two years of paring back our belongings, I'd estimate that we got rid of around 80% of our things and made ourselves a few pounds in the process (PayPal actually suspended my account because it thought I was a business, I'd flogged so much!).

As my interest in minimalism grew, Frank and I even set up our own blog, www.londonminimalists.co.uk, and I became part of a growing UK community of people who were fed up with being stuck in the vice-like grip of consumerism.

It's also through this community that I heard about Buy Nothing Day. This day falls on the same day as Black Friday, an American phenomenon that has been transported to the UK in recent years. Black Friday is the day after Thanksgiving in the US and is a popular shopping day, with consumers flocking to shopping centres to purchase deeply discounted items.

I'm making Black Friday sound much more civilised than it is. The fact that there is a website dedicated to logging the deaths and injuries that happen as a result of Black Friday shoppers squabbling over TVs and food mixers tells you all you need to know.

In the UK in 2015, Black Friday sales broke the £1 billion mark for the first time, proving that Brits can shop just as hard as our American cousins. But not everyone was out shopping. There were also those who had pledged to avoid the shops and take part in Buy Nothing Day.

Buying nothing for a day was a good start in rallying against rampant consumerism, but abstaining for a longer period would be even better for the wallet (an idea which appealed to the financial journalist in me).

But how long would a spending ban have to last to make a real impact? A week would be good, and a month would be even better, but if I really wanted to break the habit of putting my hand in my pocket and spending mindlessly then a 365-day spending ban was surely the way to go.

I decided that I was going to be one of those people who bought nothing but, instead of avoiding the shops for a single day, I was going to do it for a whole year, starting on Black Friday of 2015, 27 November.

The No Spend Year Challenge was born.

THE RULES

Every challenge has to have rules, and mine were pretty simple: I couldn't spend money on anything other than my normal bills and food.

Before I go into what I couldn't spend money on, let me tell you about what I did spend money on.

These are the total monthly outgoings for our household, which Frank and I split evenly.

Mortgage
Money to charity
Council tax

Gas and electricity
Phone bills
Water services
House and contents insurance
Money to help family
Life insurance
Critical illness insurance
Washing machine insurance
TV licence
Internet
Bank account fee

£1,896.76 TOTAL

As we divide the bills in half, my share comes to £948.38 a month – or, put in a completely more terrifying way, a huge £11,380.56 a year. Gulp.

The only other thing left to buy was food and toiletries, but more on that later.

Everything else was off-limits. Which meant there'd be no more rounds of drinks purchased in the pub (tap water only from now on), no new clothes, no presents for my nephews, no takeaway coffees, no meals out and no holidays.

There was also no budget for transport, not even a bus fare, so I'd have to go everywhere on my trusty bike.

You name it, I couldn't buy it. And I couldn't let Frank or anyone else pay for me either. That meant no drinks bought for me at the pub, no family paying for dinners out or gig tickets: it was a year of no spending, not a year of scrounging off my friends and family. That would be one way to lose mates quickly.

It was going to be hard. In order to succeed I needed a target, something to work towards. And what better target than the enormous mortgage debt hanging over our heads?

You see, when we climbed the property ladder we didn't just

end up with more spare rooms; we ended up with a bigger mortgage too.

What I thought was dizzying excitement from our house purchase was actually vertigo from standing on the top of an even larger debt pile. A debt pile that at the start of the challenge totalled a terrifying £230,091. That's right, nearly a quarter of a million quid of debt.

Considering the average mortgage debt in the UK is £85,000, according to 2015 figures from the Bank of England, I think you'll agree I've done a stellar job of putting myself in the red.

And that debt was due to hang over my head for twenty-five years.

The mortgage has always been a black cloud for me and I had made an effort in the past to chip away at it each month on the advice of a financial adviser a couple of years ago, even if it meant overpaying £50 a month.

Thanks to my job as a freelance personal finance journalist, I have access to people who know a lot about money. A few years ago the adviser told me that it makes sense to pay off your mortgage quickly and, when your mortgage is gone, throw all the spare money you no longer need to use to pay off your mortgage into a pension.

This seemed really sensible to me but the problem is that while I was overpaying the mortgage a little bit, I was still spending money like it was going out of fashion.

Don't get me wrong, I wasn't running up bucketloads of credit card debts or prioritising shopping over paying bills – Frank and I saved £6,000 in the year before the no spend year and put it into an emergency fund just in case we ever needed it.

You can see why I felt like I had a handle on my finances. But I was wrong. The reality of the situation was that I was constantly handing over my card with no real idea of how much I was spending.

A coffee in the morning, a sandwich at lunchtime, drinks after work, maybe a little treat for myself because I worked so hard – it all adds up; I just had no idea how much it was adding up to.

If you'd have asked me if I was good with money, I would have said 'Of course!' and I'm sure my friends and family would have said the same.

Day-to-day spending was compounded by the fact that I love travelling and holidays were the way I treated myself (conveniently forgetting about all the other smaller treats I gave myself throughout the year).

With the idea of a no spend year firmly entrenched in my mind, I decided to look at my bank statements to see just where my money went. You can imagine my shock when I went through a year's worth of statements and categorised everything that I'd spent, right down to the £12.50 I spent on an eye test. And I can tell you that I thought I needed another eye test when I totalled up the numbers – surely that couldn't be right! I definitely needed time off from spending.

It's a terrifying exercise but I would recommend that everyone does it. You don't need to look through a year of bank statements; looking at your spending over the past month would probably be enough to help you identify where your spending pitfalls are.

I'll divulge the embarrassing details of my spending throughout this book, and hopefully you'll be encouraged to examine your spending habits too (I'm sure they can't be as bad as mine).

THE TARGET

By enforcing a total spending ban on myself I was hoping I'd break the bad habits I had got into such as failing to set myself a spending budget, ignoring my bank statements and spending without thinking, but I also wanted to save money.

As a freelancer my money can be up and down, so I never

really knew how much I had to spend (another reason why my thoughtless spending was so silly) or how much I had to save.

For this challenge I knew the goal had to be simple: save as much as I could.

Now I know some of you will be thinking that after a year of not spending I would be desperate to treat myself: go wild in the shops or go on a once-in-a-lifetime holiday; and the thought had crossed my mind too.

Except, I'm trying to be more sensible with my cash and think more about my future.

You've seen what we pay out for from our list of bills and, unsurprisingly, our mortgage repayment makes up the majority of our outgoings.

I figure that if I can pay off my mortgage than the world will be my oyster. If I didn't have a mortgage, our outgoings would be minimal, and I would have more money in my pocket to go on holiday, or save, or we could cut down on our working hours, take up volunteer work, and generally enjoy ourselves more.

Paying off my mortgage will give financial freedom that I've never had, and I would rather have financial freedom over a new pair of shoes.

Overpaying a mortgage, even by just a small amount each month, quickly adds up. It's what's known as the 'snowball' effect.

The more money you pay in, the smaller the balance on your debt, which means you pay less interest, which means more of your monthly repayments go towards the balance, which gets smaller, and so it goes on.

Let me explain:

Imagine a mortgage of £200,000, paid back over 25 years, at an interest rate of 3%.

This means the monthly mortgage payments would be £948. That monthly payment is effectively split into two parts; one part pays the interest on the loan, and the other repays the capital (the original £200,000).

Of the £948 paid each month, £500 would go to interest and £448 would go to capital. This means that, after the first month of paying your mortgage, you would only have paid off £448 of the total £200,000 – that's why mortgages have such long terms.

If you want to know how much of your debt repayments goes towards paying down the interest and how much is capital repayment then you can follow this formula:

Interest rate/12 x the balance of your debt = interest paid
Total payment – interest paid = capital repayment
In the case above:
3.0/12 X 200,000 = 50,000 (interest = £500.00)
£948 – £500 = £448 (capital repayment)
(Note that this isn't an exact science but a rough estimate)

As the balance goes down, more of the monthly payment goes towards the capital and less towards the interest; this is how the payments 'snowball'.

The fact that such a huge amount of the mortgage payment we make every month services just the interest is quite frustrating – for me, that's wasted money.

The only ways to pay less interest are to either get a new mortgage with a lower interest rate or overpay like mad. As we're on a fixed deal, for us it'll have to be the latter.

Of course, overpaying doesn't just mean you're paying less interest; you're also cutting the term of your mortgage, or in other words paying it off much quicker.

Going back to our example of the £200,000 mortgage, if you paid the set amount of £948 for the whole 25 years of the mortgage you would pay back a total of £284,478.

That's £84,478 in interest.

However, if you overpaid £200 a month the total paid back would be £262,870, saving yourself £21,608 in interest payments.

You'd also be mortgage-free much quicker as you would pay

it off five years and 11 months earlier, taking the term of the mortgage from 25 years to 19 years.

If you ramped up the overpayments, the money you save will rise and the term of the mortgage will reduce.

Snowballing doesn't just work with mortgages, it can be applied to all debt. Let's take the example of someone with credit card debt.

Under government rules the minimum payment you have to make each month on a credit card is 1% of the total balance plus interest plus any fees, but paying it off at the minimum is going to take for ever.

Our shopper has spent £5,000 on their credit card, which has an interest rate of 18.9% APR (this stands for 'annual percentage rate' or how much it will cost each year to borrow the money spent on the card).

The minimum monthly repayment that our shopper has to make is £123.

Even if our shopper buys nothing else with the card, the total amount they will have to pay back is a staggering £12,077.

This is made up of the original £5,000 spent plus £7,077 in total interest. It's a lot of money and it takes a long time to pay off at the minimum level: 31 years and ten months to be precise. Ouch.

Compound interest?

Albert Einstein described compound interest as the 'eighth wonder of the world' and everyone who is interested in clearing debt and saving more should know about it.

The flip side of the debt coin is saving, and we all know that if we spend less money on going out then our savings pot will grow. But there is another way that your savings grow without you actually doing anything.

Compound interest could revolutionise your savings. What exactly did Einstein find so wondrous about it? It may not sound like a particularly sexy term but it's very important.

Compound interest or, more simply, compounding can transform your finances for the better.

If you have £100 saved in the bank and you're earning 3% interest each year, by the end of the first year you'll have £103 in the bank. If you continue earning 3% on your savings, by the end of the second year you'll earn £3.09. That's because you earn interest on the interest you've made.

This is compounding working for you and the bigger the sums you save, the more interest you make and the more interest you make on that interest, in a virtuous saving circle.

This, dear readers, is one of the ways the rich get richer.

Whether it's paying off a mortgage or a credit card, I think we can agree that we'd all like to be rid of our debt as soon as possible. Without the weight of debt hanging over us, we would no longer be a slave to our bills.

By applying minimalism to my mortgage debt the aim is to get rid of my largest outgoing as quickly as possible. In order to achieve that goal I also have to apply minimalism to my spending.

Of course, a year of no spending wasn't going to allow me to pay off the entirety of my huge mortgage (unfortunately I don't earn that much) but I wanted it to kick-start a new relationship with money – one where I was in control.

With twelve months of frugality ahead of me I had to keep my eye on the bigger prize. If I could get closer to financial freedom, instead of living to work and pay off debt, I'd be working to live the life I'd always wanted.

THE
NO
SPEND
YEAR

THE ▪
GROCERY ▪
CHALLENGE

I looked at the apples. Six of them lined up in their little tray. And then I looked back at the price: £1.99.

As I weighed them up in my hand I heard Frank bellowing from further down the aisle: 'STOP. Think about it! Look at the price of 'em, put 'em back.'

The well-turned-out mum behind me looked aghast. I'm sure she was wondering why I stayed with such an awful man, and one who seemed to be a complete miser.

But it wasn't what it seemed; the mission was to spend as little as possible on a weekly shop, and at £1.99 those apples weren't making it into the basket.

When setting out on the no spend challenge, my aim was to opt out of consuming for twelve months, but there are some costs in life that simply aren't optional.

I've already set out all my monthly outgoings but there was one other thing that is impossible to go without: food.

As part of the challenge, I'd have to keep my grocery spending each week to a minimum. Discussing a 'sensible' weekly grocery budget with friends and with people online was an interesting exercise.

The majority of people concluded that a weekly budget of

between £30 and £50, to cover three meals a day, snacks and drinks as well as all toiletries and cleaning products for the home, was fair.

Never one to shy away from a challenge (as you may have already guessed), I thought £50 a week was far too much and so gave myself a £30-a-week grocery budget.

Up to this point, Frank had been supportive of my challenge – bar a little bit of exasperated eye-rolling – but he went one step further when it came to groceries. While he wouldn't be doing the complete no spend year, he agreed to take part in the grocery challenge.

This meant we had to cover three meals each a day (or forty-two meals a week) plus drinks, snacks, and tea for both of us for the smallest sum possible.

On top of that we'd still have to buy toiletries (I'm sure our colleagues would say deodorant and soap were essentials!) and also cleaning products for our home, as well as washing powder for our clothes.

It was nice to have someone to do this part of the challenge with, firstly because I wasn't (and I'm still not) a very skilled or adventurous cook, and secondly because it would become such a huge part of our lives thanks to all the planning, shopping and marathon cooking sessions needed to keep the costs down.

Any reductions we made to our weekly food bill would be an improvement. Although we had tried for years to stick to a grocery budget each month, the truth is that we always spent a lot more than we had planned on food shopping.

I calculated how much we spent on food shops in the twelve months before the no spend challenge.

The total from our joint account, which we used for the bulk of our food spending, was roughly £1,850, more than we spend on council tax for the whole year.

That's not so bad, I hear you say. But wait, there's more.

When I added up the total ad hoc food spending totals from

my own account it came to another £1,000 a year. This figure also doesn't include eating out.

The £1,000 figure really stuck in my throat. This was the cost of all the times I couldn't be bothered to spend ten minutes making lunch for work and bought a sandwich instead. It was all the times I had popped into a local shop to buy something for that night's dinner and somehow spent £10.

In short, it was the price I was paying for being lazy and disorganised.

It's at this point that I should also admit to another vice that fits into the general food theme: buying coffee.

Another tally of my spending reveals that I spent £400 on coffee in just one year. That's £7.60 a week on average.

I'm not even a huge coffee fan. I'm not someone who obsesses about roasts and frothiness of milk. How had I spent that much?

Well, the answer to that question is: quite easily, and without thinking.

I had a long way to go to curb my food and drink spending habits (in fact we both did) but at least we had some figures to work from for our grocery challenge. Whatever reductions we made would be an improvement on the off-the-cuff, willy-nilly way of buying groceries we had.

CUTTING THE FOOD BILL

I'm not going to lie to you, getting our food bill down took *a lot* of effort. In fact, it became a military operation, but once you get the hang of it, it becomes second nature to shop in a way that saves money (and I promise, you'll even get a thrill out of keeping down the total on your receipt).

We decided to shop once a week (usually on a Saturday morning) and get everything we needed for the entire week. That meant none of the top-up shops that had been costing us so much money before.

There was only one opportunity to get all of our grub for the week – if we missed something off the list, we missed out until the next week.

But before we get to the shopping part of the week, let me explain the food shop routine from the beginning.

Step 1: preparation, preparation, preparation

Fail to prepare, and prepare to go hungry! That has become the motto in our house.

Before you even set foot in a supermarket, you need to take stock of what you already have. Go through your cupboards and work out exactly what's in them and what sorts of meals you can already make.

I did a huge audit of our cupboards and found rogue bags of pasta and random spices lurking at the back. I made sure we used up what we had first and then I was able to start afresh.

Now that I have a running tally of what's in the cupboards and can tell you which staple items – like rice, potatoes and veg – are about to run out, it means I don't buy doubles of items as I used to before.

As we shop weekly and revisit the cupboards regularly, it's easy to see what we're running low on. In an ideal world what would save us even more money is if we bulk-bought staple items, but as we don't have a car, instead walking to our local supermarket, it's not really an option.

Eating the food you already have may seem like an obvious idea, but how many times have you had a cupboard full of food and still popped to the local mini-supermarket and bought a pizza or some pasta?

I know that I used to stare at the contents of my cupboards waiting for some Nigella-style inspiration to hit me, only to close the door and head to Tesco Metro to buy something I could sling in the oven.

That's all changed.

Now, the weekly shop begins with a session of meal planning where we work out what we're going to eat for breakfast, lunch and dinner each week.

It may sound a bit time-consuming but it's a foolproof way to keep costs low, and the only way to make sure we don't go hungry.

Once we knew what we were going to eat, we could work out what we needed to buy.

Step 2: the list

Supermarkets want us to spend, and they're designed to make us trawl the aisles so the maximum number of things catch our eye and we are encouraged to buy them.

Shopping without a list makes us more susceptible to the lure of an offer or treating ourselves to something we don't actually need. For example, bakeries are placed near the front of the store as the smells activate our salivary glands and before you know it, some croissants are in the trolley. Similarly, always cast your eyes down the rows of shelves; the products the supermarkets want you to buy – i.e. the most expensive, branded ones – are at eye level while the cheaper versions tend to be displayed lower down.

In the days before I went shopping with a list I would often wander round the supermarket, aimlessly chucking things in the trolley and not thinking about whether I was putting together an actual meal. This usually meant I'd be back to the shop topping up later in the week.

The beauty of a shopping list is that you can also estimate just how much the weekly shop will cost you, which is particularly handy if you're working to a budget or, like us, trying to get the costs down to the bare minimum.

In short, treat your trolley like a fancy nightclub, of which you're the bouncer: if it's not on your shopping list, it's not getting in!

Step 3: forget loyalty

Your regular supermarket might send you the odd money-off coupon or even give you free coffee, but that doesn't mean they deserve your unwavering loyalty; they only do those things to keep you coming back.

The trick to keeping your shopping bill low is to shop around and constantly compare prices.

We used to shop in Sainsbury's, purely for convenience as it was the big supermarket that was closest to us. I dread to think how much money we squandered in there over the years.

If we had continued to shop there exclusively I know we wouldn't have been able to reduce our food bill by half as much; instead we made the simple choice to shop around on our local high street.

Now the main bulk of our shopping is done at discount supermarket Lidl, where the prices are a fraction of those charged by Sainsbury's and other major supermarkets too, for that matter, but the quality is just as good – even when it comes to fruit and veg, which I must admit I was sceptical about at first.

But our shop doesn't just stop there, because Lidl doesn't have an exhaustive list of products like larger brand-name supermarkets do. Also on our high street is a smaller Sainsbury's, which we used every week, and a Chinese supermarket that was great for cheap spices, herbs, and tofu (we don't eat meat – which is another way to keep food costs down).

As well as sticking with budget supermarkets, it's worth keeping a loose tally of the costs of the items you buy the most, as prices can fluctuate, as well as trying not to be swept up by what seem like unbeatable offers, like 3 for 2 or BOGOF (buy one get one free) deals.

The 'deals' you see in supermarkets are not always good value for money, especially for perishable items. If you won't eat the extra bag of oranges you got in the BOGOF it won't be worth it. But keep an eye out for deals on staple items and expensive products such as washing powder.

As well as ditching any supermarket loyalty, loyalty to any particular brands should be put by the wayside.

It's amazing how many times someone will say: 'I'd never buy anything but Heinz beans' and then quite happily eat own-brand ones without knowing.

Branding doesn't make the food tastier, it just makes it more expensive and own-brand products are often just as good. I'm not saying you have to only buy the very cheapest 'basics' brands, but dropping just one brand down could make you sizeable savings.

Step 4: batch cooking

If you visited our house on a Saturday around midday, it's likely that you'd find a huge cooking pot on the hob, and it would probably have one of three meals bubbling away in it: chilli, Bolognese, or a curry (all veggie as neither of us eats meat).

We stuck with these three meals on rotation for almost the whole year, bar one week where I made a stew that didn't go quite to plan.

These huge vats of food – known as batch cooking – are what we prepare for lunch for the following week.

Once cooked, the food is decanted into plastic containers and put in the freezer, ready for us to take to work.

Cheap? Yes. Easy? Undoubtedly. Boring? Most definitely.

Eating the same thing for lunch every day is dull, there's absolutely no getting away from that (although I know people who buy the same meal deal sandwich every day), but it is a brilliant way to cut costs.

Not only does cooking food in bulk work out at better value than cooking day to day, it saves even more money by keeping you out of the shops at lunchtimes.

I started to see my midday meal purely as fuel to get me around on my bike; thinking like this meant that it didn't really matter what that fuel was.

To break up the monotony, our dinners are more varied. They can be anything from stir fry to home-made falafel, as long as it's cheap and filling.

There is a huge amount of resources out there when it comes to cheap recipes. Jack Monroe's *Cooking on a Bootstrap* is a fantastic place to start and the BBC Good Food website has 'Cheap eats' recipes.

Let's say you do something that thousands of people do every working day; you spend £3 on a meal deal, which includes a sandwich, packet of crisps and a drink.

If you work five days a week, for forty-eight weeks a year (factoring in holidays), those meal deals (which, let's be honest, aren't that tasty and are probably not that good for you either) cost you:

£720 a year!

Now let's compare that to the cost of making it yourself. As I've had a lot of time on my hands this year, I've worked out the costs of my lunchtime, batch-cooked meals:

Chilli and rice: 58p

Spaghetti Bolognese: 45p

Curry and rice: 52p

Meaning the average cost of my lunch is 51p per day, or £122.40 a year.

That's a saving of £597.60!

What could you do with nearly £600? A nice holiday, a second-hand car?

What you might dismiss as 'only three quid' adds up over the course of a year. Of course, you probably don't want to cost all your meals quite as obsessively as I have, but you can be sure that home-made will work out cheaper than ready-made.

A week of shopping

To give you an idea of what we spend our money on for a week, and what we eat, the following is a breakdown of a shopping trip and the subsequent week of food.

We don't need to buy every single ingredient for every dinner each week as there are oils and herbs in the cupboards left over from previous shopping trips, and half bags of bits like lentils and rice that we try to use up.

The shop

8 x tinned tomatoes (31p each) £2.48

Jar peanut butter £1.18

2 x tinned chickpeas (33p each) 66p

2 x jar sun-dried tomatoes (on sale 49p each) 98p

Clear honey £1.35

Large bottle balsamic vinegar 99p

2 x bags of pasta (29p each) 58p

Bread mix £1.09

Gravy granules 99p

Oats 39p

Chocolate chips for baking 65p

4 x large onions 85p

2.5kg potatoes £1.49

3-pack of peppers 79p

Spinach 59p

Bag of carrots 45p

Spring onions 45p

Beetroot 75p

Kitchen roll £1.48

Foil 67p

14 bananas £2.14

2 x garlic bulbs (30p each) 60p

4 x soya milk (85p each) £3.40

1 x almond milk £1

Margarine £1.20
Frozen berries £2.20
2 x tubs of mushrooms (£1 each) £2
2 x loose parsnips 54p
375g soya mince £1.89
2 x tofu blocks £2.80

Total = £36.63

What we did with it:
Breakfasts: either oats or smoothies
Lunches: a batch-cooked spaghetti Bolognese
Dinners: pasta, tofu scramble with potatoes, falafel and salad, and a stew

It's not the most interesting of meal plans, I grant you, but it's filling and it's cheap. I also managed to squeeze out of the budget a batch of biscuits, which were perfect for a quick energy boost before a bike ride.

GETTING FREE GRUB

A no spend year wasn't about seeing what I could scrounge for free from friends and family, but there are ways to get free food that won't lose you mates.

The growing trend for 'zero food waste' has led to a proliferation of various food-sharing apps and groups.

One that I found particularly useful was Olio. It's essentially a local listing of food (mostly, although it does also carry other items) that people are giving away — maybe they've had a glut at an allotment or are going on holiday and don't want to put their salad in the bin. You can sort the food for offer by area and pick up items that are conveniently located.

It's good for your wallet and for the environment.

I also listed a few bits and pieces I had in the cupboards that I didn't actually know how to cook with and which, to be honest, I'd bought on a whim because they seemed like trendy ingredients (buckwheat, anyone?). Hopefully the person who picked up my offering was a better cook than me.

There's also another way to get food for nothing, although it might not be everyone's cup of tea.

One of our best finds happened by chance after an evening out at a free lecture at the London School of Economics.

Walking back to our bikes we passed a bakery with piles of white bin bags sitting outside, one of which had been ripped open. Sticking out of the hole was a baguette. On further inspection, the bag was stuffed with all kinds of bread.

It was all perfectly good and was just, I assume, left over from the day and could no longer be sold. Piles of baguettes, olive bread and rustic-looking loaves – the kind of baked goods that cost a fortune in a fancy bakery – all sitting there for the bin man to take away.

We loaded up with an armful of baguettes, we gave the majority to some homeless people sleeping nearby and the rest we took home, where they made their way into the freezer. Our free bread lasted us for ages and now I can't cycle past a bakery after closing hours without having a quick look at what's in the bin bags.

FOOD WASTE

One unexpected bonus of the challenge was that, by being more conscious of our food spending, planning all our meals and buying only the ingredients we needed, we reduced the amount of food we wasted.

The truth is, we used to throw out bags of uneaten salad, wilting spring onions and sprouting potatoes on a regular basis purely because we were purchasing items without any idea of how we'd use them.

Now very little is wasted; even vegetables that look a little sorry for themselves have the rotten bits chopped off and are commandeered into a dish.

I'd estimate that of the food we used to buy, 20% would have been wasted. If I think of how much we used to spend on food in a year (£2,850 including top-up shops), that means we were throwing £570 a year straight in the bin.

Of course, you could bypass the shops completely and grow your own. I was gifted two tomato plants by a generous London gardener.

I'll admit, under my watch they nearly died, but after Frank took charge of them they thrived and we even managed to get some tomatoes out of them.

I envy the green-fingered; growing your own fruit and veg is a great way to keep down costs and reduce food waste.

While I'm grateful for the tomato plants, I don't think I'd go full-on *Good Life* and start growing my own. I just don't have the patience.

FUEL NOT FOOD

Planning every meal became routine, but that doesn't mean it was always easy. Although I don't like cooking, I do like eating, but I wasn't really eating for pleasure any more.

More often than not, during the challenge I was eating for just one reason: energy.

Cycling numerous miles every week meant I needed all the energy I could get, and food morphed from being something I'd hugely enjoyed to being simply a source of fuel; and I was looking for that fuel at the cheapest price. Jars of peanut butter became my best friend – but there's only so much of it one girl can eat.

I started to fantasise about proper spicy curries, big fat veggie burgers and expertly folded dim sum. My home-made chickpea burgers (which fell apart when you looked at them) and my decidedly bland curries just weren't cutting the mustard.

I missed enjoying food, but I have to admit I was eating far better than I had done before. Gone were the convenience foods and treats, replaced by green leaves and a salad drawer bursting with colour.

I was still eating well – it's not like I was tucking into a plate of gruel three times a day – I just wasn't 'treating' myself with expensive food or meals out any more.

When I thought about it properly, I realised it was the idea of the treat that I was missing more than the actual food.

The way I've eaten over the past year has been far healthier and more filling than my previous diet, and the food hasn't been bad, just monotonous at times. Would that monotony be cancelled out by the promise of a nice dinner out now and again? Yes.

Would I continue eating like this if once a month I could order a takeaway curry? Hell yes!

At the end of the day, it's all about balance. If I eat well and cheaply for the majority of the month then I won't feel bad about ordering a takeaway or going out for a meal. Plus, I'll have the money to do so because I'll have saved so much on my shopping.

IN THE HOME

We had to buy not just food but also cleaning products for our home and clothes.

I was a total sucker for brand-name laundry detergents and bleach sprays, and automatically thought that the own-brand stuff wouldn't be as good.

Pre-spending challenge I'd estimated that we easily spent £12 a month on bleaches, toilet cleaners, antibacterial sprays, laundry tablets, stain remover and fabric conditioner, as well as sponges and cloths.

We just couldn't afford to spend that £12 a month any more; but we'd still need to clean our home and our clothes.

It took a while to run down the mountain of products we'd managed to build up (the large amount of clothing detergent from our original stock was the last thing to run out, only doing so in April – five months into the challenge).

However, the Comfort fabric conditioner ran out almost immediately and so did our Vanish stain remover (I told you we liked brands).

I made the mistake of repurchasing the fabric conditioner (I didn't think about whether it was an essential until someone called me out on it on Twitter), and I didn't bother buying it again after that.

The stain remover was a different story, however. Our white towels and bed sheets started to look a little bit grey but instead of shelling out for an expensive pot of Vanish, we went for a cheaper alternative.

Online friends, when asked for a replacement, waxed lyrical about Napisan – the babycare product used for bibs, reuseable nappies, babygros and anything else that a baby uses that gets messy and stained.

Not only does the product work well and smell clean, it's also much cheaper than Vanish; at our local Sainsbury's 800g of Napisan costs £3.80 where 470g of Vanish costs £5.75. To make that comparable: 100g of Vanish costs £1.22 while 100g of Napisan costs just 47p.

I'm sure you'll agree that's a bargain. It's small changes like this, which actually don't require too much thought or planning, that will keep your money in your pocket.

Similarly, I've totally changed the way I think about the cleaning products we use in the house.

Previously I was sold on the idea that we needed separate

sprays for the different parts of the house. I was an advertiser's dream, buying bathroom cleaning products for the bathroom and buying kitchen cleaning products for the kitchen. I was buying what I was told like a good consumer.

But how different are all these liquids and sprays? The answer is, not very different at all.

After all our cleaning lotions and potions started to run out I was planning on replacing them, but just in the nick of time a casual conversation on Twitter opened my eyes.

Before I'd probably been spending £5 a month on cleaning sprays (as a conservative estimate), but now I spend just a fraction of that: a huge 17p a month.

How? The cleaning product to rule them all: white vinegar.

This ridiculously cheap product is one of the greatest finds of the whole no spend challenge and I'm glad I found it as early on as I did.

A 500ml bottle of the stuff is just 50p and lasts around three months, which breaks down to about 17p a month.

I took an empty spray bottle (of which I had plenty) and mixed a third vinegar and two-thirds water into it and *voila*! A multipurpose cleaner that makes stainless steel shine, takes limescale off the bath and makes easy work of spills.

Admittedly, your house does smell a bit like a fish and chip shop when you spray it but the smell soon dissipates. For those who really can't stand the smell, a few drops of lemon juice or an essential oil (I've heard lavender is good) help cover up the chip-shop pong.

I can honestly say that switching to vinegar as a cleaning product is one of my most exciting money-saving tips (I live an exciting life, I know!). I can't stop recommending it to people.

Not only does it actually work but it has saved us a small fortune in cleaning products: we've gone from spending £60 a year on sprays to just £2 a year.

Who doesn't want to save £58 a year, and by making such a small tweak?

In fact, all the changes we've made to the way we shop for the household are pretty small on an individual level, but add them together and they make a huge difference.

Household items are something we have to purchase and it's easy to go on to autopilot when shopping. I spent so many years as a consumer, being sold to, and this challenge has opened my eyes to that.

It might not be easy to make all the changes that I've set out in one go, but start slowly and once you feel comfortable with a change you've made, add in another.

Next week, make the effort to take your lunch to work instead of buying it, even if it's just for two days. Then you can build it into your routine.

After that, start meal planning – maybe not for the whole week at first but for a few days – and then shop (with a list) for those days.

Once you've done this a few times it will become second nature and will keep your pounds out of the tills and in your pocket.

SPENDING HACKS

Top tips for savvy shopping

Following my four steps will cut your food bill, but there are other smaller ways to help reduce your costs.

1. Aisle be damned!

Supermarkets like to hide bargains in order to get you to spend more. Spices are a great example of this. A branded 28g pot of cumin in the herbs and spices aisle of my local supermarket costs £1.35 compared to a 100g bag of cumin in the ethnic food section priced at just 75p.

This principle can also be applied to dried fruits and nuts – buying these items in the snack aisle will cost you a lot more than buying them in the baking section, as baking items are VAT-free whereas snack items are not.

2. Never shop hungry

This is a simple rule but if you go out with your tummy rumbling, you'll be much more susceptible to the goodies on offer.

I made this mistake one week while food shopping on my own. I ended up buying a bread roll (29p) and a bottle of water (19p) – even though the extra I'd spent was less than 50p I felt guilty about it (although that may just show you how far I was going in my penny-pinching ways!).

3. Multitasking ingredients

Some recipes require a list of ingredients longer than your arm, which is not only expensive but leaves you with a cupboard full of redundant half-used jars.

Cutting your food bill doesn't mean you can't try new recipes; just make sure you have more than one plan for your ingredients. This isn't just true of fancy herbs or unusual vegetables – it can also mean thinking ahead so you know that big bag of carrots will be used in a stir-fry as well as a stew.

It'll make sure your food and your money aren't wasted.

4. Take cash and a calculator

Yes, you might look a little bit bonkers adding up your shopping and ticking off your list, but who cares? You'll be the one saving money.

Before, I used to hand over my card without thinking; now I leave the cards at home and take cash to the supermarket. It stops impulse purchasing and means you are far more thoughtful about what you're spending.

I don't forget to take my loyalty cards along though to make sure I get my points on my shopping, because we all know points equal prizes!

5. Learn about portions

One of the reasons we used to waste so much food was because we would cook far too much. Now we've worked out the optimum amount for our portions (which tend to be on the large side as we both cycle so much), which means nothing ever goes to waste, and we're not eating too much either – good for wallets and for waistlines.

6. Early birds get the freshest worms

I can't stand food shopping and like to get in, get my stuff and get out. I hate it when I can't get what I want in the place I want to get it, and at the cheapest price.

We've found that getting up early to get to the shops is essential, especially at the discount supermarkets where the fresh fruit and veg tends to disappear pretty quickly.

Alternatively, if you're a night owl, find out what time your local supermarket restocks for the next day – if you work late or don't like early mornings, you may be able to hit the shops at night, before everyone else has even thought about their shopping.

7. Don't be a rock star

Rock stars never know the price of a pint of milk, but we're not rock stars and it's likely you aren't either. Know the price of your staple purchases to make sure you're always getting a good deal.

This is particularly true when there's a deal on as often supermarkets will hike a price to make a special offer seem like better value. If you know the 'normal' price then you won't be fooled into parting with more cash.

8. Invest in . . .

I'm not one for splashing the cash, obviously, but decent resealable plastic containers are something every thrifty shopper should have.

Without these we wouldn't be able to freeze and transport our lunches half as well. I'm not a huge fan of freezer bags partly because they often don't stand up to transportation and also because they're a pain to clean (you didn't think we used them once and just threw them away, did you?!).

Once you've got your plastic containers, you've got no reason not to start cooking smarter and saving money.

THE
NO
SPEND
YEAR

SAVING ■
FOR A ■
RAINY ■
DAY

SAVING FOR A RAINY DAY

Saving money is great, especially if you're going to get something nice out of it at the end, like a holiday or car.

But there is a form of saving that we should all do that isn't necessarily going to provide us with a treat, but which could potentially keep a roof over our head and food on the table.

I'm talking about the emergency buffer that we should all have to hand in case the landlord increases the rent, the boiler breaks or you lose your job.

As with most things in finance, there is a helpful rule of thumb to follow. In the case of a savings buffer, it's accepted that you should have enough put away to cover six months' bills – that's rent/mortgage, utilities, food and the other essentials.

I'd be the first to hold my hands up: six months is a lot of cash to save so three months is also acceptable – and, in all honesty, more realistic. In our household we have £6,000 saved that will cover three months of bills and food in the event that both me and Frank lose our jobs or a large unexpected expense rears its head.

An emergency buffer may be a pain to save, and it may be tempting to dip into it thinking 'It'll never happen to me' or 'I'll replace it one day', but wishful thinking won't get you very far if an emergency does crop up. Take the sting out of saving by setting up a direct debit to make a payment into a savings account when you get paid. By paying yourself first – or paying your future self first – means the money won't be sitting in your account, tempting you to spend it and you'll get used to automatically saving.

A savings buffer is especially pertinent in these uncertain times; the financial crisis of 2008 is still within recent memory and with the UK voting to leave the European Union, the future of the economy is anyone's guess. It's yet to be seen whether the UK economy will hold steady or will fall into recession, which would put jobs at risk.

It's boring and sensible but sound advice: put some money away for a rainy day.

There are plenty of other proverbial umbrellas that you can put in place for when the rain comes, in the form of insurance. What insurance suits you best will depend on your circumstances but it is worth knowing the other ways in which you can protect yourself, your income, your home and your family.

If you have a mortgage or you have dependants (children or someone you split the bills with) then it's worth thinking about whether you need some insurance. Here are the main ones to think about:

LIFE INSURANCE

What it does: pays out a lump sum or regular payments when you die.

Is it worth it?: if you have a partner or children who depend on your income to cover mortgage payments or living expenses then it could be worth it.

We have joint life insurance that pays off the mortgage if either me or Frank die, which may seem morbid, but if one of us isn't around then we want to make sure the other can continue living in the house.

CRITICAL ILLNESS

What it does: pays out a lump sum (or in some cases a regular income) if you are critically ill, for example if you have a heart attack or get certain specified types of cancer.

Is it worth it?: again it depends on whether you have

people who rely on your income and if your illness would render you unable to work, leaving your dependants in financial difficulty.

I have a critical illness policy that pays out a lump sum – enough to clear the mortgage – in the event that I become too ill to work. I wouldn't want to worry about losing my home on top of worrying about an illness.

INCOME PROTECTION

What it does: pays a percentage of your take-home pay if you can't work because of illness or disability.

Is it worth it?: it will cover your living expenses and bills if you can't work because of illness or disability, so it prevents you from ending up in poverty.

I don't actually have this insurance, but probably should, considering it's pretty much made for people who are self-employed and don't have workplace insurance to fall back on.

Before you sign up to any insurance policy, check to see if your workplace offers them; many do at a discounted rate or as part of your benefits package. If your workplace doesn't offer insurance then contact an independent insurance broker, who will be able to advise you on the policies that are best for you and find you the most suitable cover at the best price.

THE PERSONAL DEBT MOUNTAIN

In our 'buy now, pay later' society it's unusual to find anyone who hasn't put a purchase on a credit card or slipped into their overdraft on occasion.

In the past I've been guilty of letting purchases sit on a credit card racking up interest, and going into the red on my current account because I didn't want to miss out on dinner or drinks with my friends.

Sometimes putting something on credit is unavoidable, especially if you haven't got an emergency fund and an expensive emergency crops up.

Credit cards aren't all bad; many offer perks such as air miles or cashback bonuses. And if you need to build up a credit rating, credit cards are a good way to do that.

The danger with putting it on the plastic is not paying off your purchases straight away and getting stung with high interest charges, particularly on credit and store cards.

Credit card jargon

If you've got a credit card then you've probably heard of 'APR', but few people know what it means or why it's important.

APR stands for 'annual percentage rate' and is essentially the cost of borrowing over the year, so the higher the APR the higher the rate of interest you have to pay back.

However, sometimes the APR isn't what it seems. If you're anything like me then you'll get plenty of junk mail through the door offering you credit cards with 'typical' or 'representative' APRs.

These APRs are usually an OK deal but that doesn't mean you're going to get that rate. Just 51% of people have to qualify for a rate for it to be 'typical'. So with just half of people qualifying that means you have a good chance of ending up paying a rate that is higher than the one you're being advertised.

It's a bit of a catch-22 when it comes to credit cards because you won't know what rate you'll get until you apply, but every time you apply for a credit card a 'footprint' is left on your credit file. The more footprints you have, the less likely you are to get the most advantageous rates. The best thing you can do is check your credit rating before you apply for a credit card; the better your credit score, the better your chance of getting the cheaper APR.

The cost of credit

The average APR on a credit card hit a record high in March 2016 of 21.6% according to comparison website Moneyfacts. This means for every £1,000 spent on the credit card, you'd pay £216 in interest each year.

If you pay your credit card balance off at the end of the month you'll avoid paying interest. This is the best way to use credit cards.

But not everyone does this; many people choose to pay the minimum amount they can get away with each month. This is the worst way to use credit cards.

Let's take the example of a super-spender who is planning a dream holiday.

It costs them £1,000. They put it on their credit card, which has an average APR of 21.6%, and then they choose to pay the minimum amount on their card each month.

According to the small print in their contract, their credit card company works out the minimum payment as 1% of the money owed plus interest or £5, whichever is highest.

Based on this calculation, our holidaymaker will have to pay £27 in repayments in the first month but the minimum payment will decrease over time as the balance comes down (as long as they don't purchase any more).

Paying the £1,000 holiday off at the minimum rate means our sun-seeker would be in for a long haul.

Paying off the minimum (and remember, they're not using the card to buy any more) means it would take them a staggering 18 years and 11 months to pay back the £1,000.

And because it's taken so long the interest they pay would exceed the cost of the holiday at £1,441.

Added together, the total cost of the holiday would be £2,441.

This is an extreme example but it just shows how much interest can cost you.

Let's say that our holidaymaker sticks with the original minimum payments of £27 a month instead of reducing the minimum payment.

The holiday would still take four years and ten months to pay back and the interest would total £553, adding 50% to the cost of the holiday.

We all like a week away now and again but saving for a holiday – or any other treat – is the best way to go unless you want to be paying for it long after your tan has faded.

If you want to work out just how much your credit card debt will cost you, visit www.cardcost.org.uk, which is run by the credit card trade association UK Cards Association.

THE
NO
SPEND
YEAR

GOODBYE
SOCIAL LIFE?
FINDING NEW
WAYS TO
HAVE FUN

'Now that everyone has a card, could you all stand up and place your cards on the altar,' said the woman in Aztec print harem trousers standing at the front of the room.

I glanced at my friend Rowan as we stood up, along with around twenty other women, and made our way to the altar, adorned with candles and, inexplicably, a teddy bear.

Just twenty minutes previously we'd walked through the door to take part in a women's sacred circle and had already been 'cleansed' with incense and each had picked a card depicting an animal.

'Now shake it out,' ordered the woman as tribal music started to play. 'I want you to feel your animal. If you have fur, feel the fur. If you have wings, feel the air beneath them.'

And this is how I found myself trying to create an interpretative dance inspired by my animal: the wild boar.

For the next hour and a half of my life I made a total idiot of myself scrabbling around on the floor trying to mimic a boar.

It was the longest hour and a half of my life.

That's the thing with having no budget for going out; you have to take your fun where you can find it.

And the women's sacred circle was definitely an, er . . . experience. I don't think I've ever laughed as hard in my life.

Over the past year I've done a lot of things in the pursuit of fun that I wouldn't have done before. It would have been easy to not spend any money by sitting indoors for a year, but the aim of the game was to see if I could still live my life, including having a social life, without spending.

Embarrassingly, my social life before the no spend year revolved around the pub. And eating. And then back to the pub again.

In fact, my bank statements from the year before the challenge show that I spent £1,570 in the pub! (Not that I can remember much of it.)

Not only is it shameful that I spent so much money on pints, it's also a bit sad that I've wasted so much time looking at the inside of different boozers, but I can see how it happens.

I don't know if it's the same for you but I work long hours and the people I want to spend my free time with also work long hours. They're busy and they're knackered and all they want to do at the end of the day is plonk themselves down in a comfy seat with a glass of wine and have a chat. In all fairness, I think this is the recipe for a great night.

And if we weren't heading for a drink, we'd be going for dinner – another prime place for spending (too much) money. Another tally of my restaurant spending for a year makes a stomach-churning £1,110.

On the bright side, at least I knew from the start I'd be able to save £2,680 (booze + restaurants) because these places wouldn't be an option for me any more.

That said, and although I wouldn't be spending any money there, it doesn't mean I managed to avoid the pub altogether.

Just because I couldn't drink didn't mean my friends were all of a sudden about to renounce their love of a night on the tiles; I kept ending up there, drinking my pint of tap water and listening to people get louder and drunker. It was frustrating to say the least.

The truth is, the first four months of the no spend year were frustrating and on more than one occasion I wished I hadn't bothered starting.

It wasn't just the fact that I couldn't drink; it was that going out, something that was so easy before when I spent ridiculous amounts of money on it, had become a chore.

Everything was harder than I thought it would be: for a start, with my challenge beginning in November it was bloody cold. No one wants to go out when it's raining and blowing a gale.

If I had to choose between a cosy night by a roaring pub fire or taking a street art tour on a wet Wednesday evening, I know which I'd choose.

Secondly, I had to cycle to meet my friends in the dark and the rain, which made everything harder. I'd turn up soaking wet or freezing cold, or both.

One night in January particularly sticks in my mind. I'd arranged with a group of friends to see Lumiere London, an outdoor light festival, which involved walking around the city looking at different light installations.

We had planned to meet by Westminster Abbey, which had been illuminated, and then wander to Oxford Street to see a few more, then up again to King's Cross. The problem was it was just four degrees that evening and by the time I'd met my friends I'd been cycling for an hour. Despite leggings under my jeans and two jumpers under my jacket, I was frozen through, and the two pairs of socks hadn't prevented my toes from going numb.

I was miserable and after a couple of hours I couldn't stand it any more and left. Even the flask of tea I'd brought with me wasn't helping.

I had images of all my nights out for the next year ending in me going home early, or me being cold, or me being the only one not drunk, or me being – let's be frank – really bloody boring.

And that was it: more than I was worried about not having fun, I was worried about people thinking I was boring. I was worried that if I wasn't fitting into conventional social situations people wouldn't want to hang out with me.

For a long time it really felt like that and each time plans were cancelled (usually because of the weather) I felt more isolated and more excluded. A plan being cancelled wasn't something I'd have worried about before – I'd have just rearranged – but in this odd new world of trying to maintain a social life I started to take the cancellations personally, feeling that they were somehow proof of my fears that people didn't want to go out with someone who wasn't spending money. Going out was the only thing I had to look forward to, so when I couldn't go, I felt it hard.

I'd never really thought about 'social conventions' before, I'd always just gone with the flow. If there was a birthday party, I'd go. If there was a gig, I'd go. If a new restaurant opened, count me in. Impromptu night out on the tiles, yes please.

In short, I had always fitted in. Suddenly not fitting in was hard to get my head round.

I wanted to hibernate, to stay away from social situations where I felt awkward, and in the first three months of the year I took on more work to distract me from the fact that I wasn't going out.

In the bubble of my challenge, when I was on my own or with Frank, it didn't seem too bad. But throw in other people and the challenge became far more difficult. I didn't have control over how people spent their time and it was difficult to think of myself as an outsider.

I hadn't prepared myself to feel like this, and I had no idea I would care so much about feeling that way. I knew the challenge would be hard – it wouldn't be a challenge otherwise – but there was a big fat monetary reward waiting at the end. However, the reward didn't seem to matter when I felt miserable and left out. Dealing with those feelings was one of the hardest parts of the challenge.

But then something happened. The flowers started to bloom, the days got a little bit longer, and everyone seemed to rub their eyes and venture out into the sunshine. Spring was here!

The world looked different and suddenly something clicked. I realised exactly what I was doing wrong.

I'd been trying to live my old life without any money and it was a plan doomed to failure. My old social life involved spending money on gig tickets, theatre tickets, cinema trips and nice meals out. It was ridiculous to think I'd be able to carry on in the same vein.

I made the decision to stop hankering after my old life and embrace the new life that having no budget presented me with. And do you know what, there's a lot of free stuff out there if you can be bothered to look for it.

THE GREAT OUTDOORS

One of the first changes I made was to do more things that were, by their very nature, free. This involved going outside. A lot.

Encouraged by the good weather (and a 100-mile bike ride for charity), I got out on my bike weekend after weekend for training rides, sometimes just me and Frank but often with friends who love cycling too. It was a fantastic way to see mates, get my training in and see some beautiful countryside.

I went on more walks in my local area, taking water and a flask of tea and using the time to catch up with friends. It's amazing what you learn about people when you have time to really listen and chat to them. Of course, you think you know a lot about your friends' lives but a lot gets lost in translation when you communicate via texts and snatched evenings in noisy restaurants.

Often people are so busy that you don't see them for weeks on end and, when you do, you're trying to fit so many anecdotes and updates into a short time frame that you don't get time to actually delve deeper into what's going on in their lives, both the good and the bad.

Having nothing to distract us, like a gig or a play, meant we had no choice but to talk and it was eye-opening.

In the spirit of getting outdoors, I took up the offer to go wild swimming with a colleague. Not only did I make a new friend but I had an exhilarating experience swimming (for free) out in nature. I have always enjoyed swimming, both in the sea and in the local pool, and can't believe it's taken me this long to dip my toe into the wild swimming phenomenon. Rather than trudge to the pool to swim in chlorine, you swim in nature's pools, whether that be a river, a lake or a creek.

I absolutely loved my first dip in Hampstead Ponds (despite having lived in London for a decade and visited Hampstead Heath many times, I had yet to take the plunge) but I was surprised by how many people turned their noses up at it. If it didn't have chlorine and a designated deep end, they didn't want to know.

It's funny what you get used to; you'd think that by reducing my going-out budget to zero I'd have closed off my options for having fun. But instead I felt that I expanded them because I had to be far more creative and resourceful. If I had money to spend on swimming, I've have paid to visit the local pool, but without money I was forced to think again and ended up enjoying swimming in a totally different way.

FOOD FOR THOUGHT

Luckily, people were more open to finding new ways to hang out if food was still involved. Of course, restaurants were off the menu but I could still make food for myself and others.

I'm not a great cook and a lack of confidence meant I didn't often ask people over for dinner. If I wanted to break bread with my friends then I'd have to get over my fear of poisoning everyone with my dreadful cooking.

And I did get over it, thanks to a few faithful recipes that I churned out time and time again. I'd say we had people round for dinner two or three times a month, working on a rotation of friends. I'd do the cooking and they'd bring wine – which I was always happy to accept.

Then they'd reciprocate and invite us round for a meal but, here's the rub, I couldn't bring booze. So I replaced the bottle of wine with cake. And if I hadn't had time to bake a cake, I'd do all the washing-up.

Although this was a neat solution, there were times when I felt quite awkward brandishing a squashed cake that had spent the journey over in my rucksack. It's not an ideal gift for the hosts.

A squashed cake isn't as awkward as the times I did get stuck in a restaurant with friends, unable to eat. The first was a New Year's Day walk that turned into a pub lunch. I sat wedged in the middle of the table with my pint of tap water while everyone chomped through hearty dinners and puddings.

To say I felt a bit daft when the waiter went to take my order and I had to tell him I wasn't eating is an understatement. And to say I wasn't envious of all the lovely food that piled up on the table would be a lie. Of course, my generous friends would have paid for me, but the point of a no spend year isn't getting your mates to sub you so it was water for me that day.

I ran into a similar problem when meeting a friend's parents who were visiting from Australia. Once again, being stuck in a lovely restaurant having to eschew the very tempting meals was hard on my stomach, even though I'd eaten before I met them. I'm sure I made a rather odd impression on my friend's parents, even though they knew why I wasn't eating with everyone else.

Thankfully, I didn't have to make a nuisance of myself in

restaurants too many times and my friends were great when it came to inventive ways to have dinner together.

We even managed to have dinner 'out' by making use of the public spaces London has to offer. London is an expensive place and meeting up with friends usually cost something, even if it was just the price of a coffee. I was resigned to shelling out money if I wanted to plonk myself down somewhere.

Now I make use of the fantastic and free public areas in the capital, often frequenting the Barbican and the Royal Festival Hall. Not only are they great to pop to in the daytime and a good space to work from thanks to the free Wi-Fi, but due to their late opening hours they became makeshift restaurants for me and my friends.

I'd bring some food from home, my friends would typically bring their dinner that they'd grabbed on the way, and we'd spend hours chatting and eating together. With the moody lighting, the hustle and bustle, and the trendy furniture, it was almost as if we were in a restaurant (albeit without the hefty bill at the end).

Over the summer we even dined al fresco, making use of the long days and London's beautiful parks to eat together outside. Normally I'd have spent a fortune buying lots of snacks and picnic food, but with a limited budget my standard contribution to the picnic became falafel salad, which thankfully everyone loves (or were too polite to say they didn't) and doesn't cost an arm and a leg.

Sharing food, and sharing the burden of providing food, kept costs low not just in the park but also for large group dinners. I love having people round to my house to eat and hang out and I was concerned that I wouldn't be able to have large groups of friends over because it would push my food budget up too high. There's a simple solution: everyone brings a dish.

For a pre-Christmas get-together at my house I made a pie and a couple of vegetable side dishes and friends brought more pies and sides, home-made bread and dessert. We were all stuffed, had a lovely time together and it didn't cost any of us a fortune.

I was quite worried when I started the challenge that our house would become a no-go zone for our friends, devoid of cheer. I was concerned they'd think of our household as miserly; a place they wouldn't get fed and watered.

In reality I had nothing to fear. Rather than people avoiding our joyless home, I found people were more willing to come round. They knew I couldn't go to the pub so they were happy to pop round for dinner; and more local friends made more unexpected stop-offs for cups of tea and a chat.

They know the kettle is always on and I really enjoyed how the house became a more social hub, with a stream of people coming in and out. My fears about not seeing anyone were quickly allayed – I actually started to see more of people and a greater breadth of people too.

LEAVING THE COMFORT ZONE

Without the fallback going-out solution of my pre-challenge life, I had to make more effort not only to see people but also to keep an open mind about what we might end up doing.

Before, I was happy to go along with the status quo for a standard Saturday night out, and I'd go as far as to say I enjoyed doing the same thing time and again. I figured that I worked hard, my free time was precious, and so doing things I knew I enjoyed was a good idea. Why would I waste money trying something that I might not enjoy, and waste my free time in the process?

It's a ridiculous way to think but does illustrate how much of a rut I'd got myself into. If I wanted to have a fun night out during the challenge I would have to shake off this negative mindset and be far more open to trying new things.

That's how my friend Rowan and I ended up in a women's sacred circle pretending to be a wild boar and a hawk respectively. There's not a chance that I would have gone to the 'spiritual awakening' event if I had had money to spend – although in all honesty I don't think I'll be going back!

I feel very differently about a creative thinking and mindfulness workshop that I attended, run by my friend Emma. Another friend, Trina, and I agreed to be guinea pigs for Emma, who wanted to try out new activities for a course she hoped to start.

To say I was apprehensive was an understatement. I was very nervous about throwing myself into an activity that I had no clue about and I felt completely out of my depth. The workshop was pretty intense and involved lots of emotional discussions as well as storytelling, art and meditation.

If you had told me a few years ago that I would spend a day meditating and discussing the texture and smells of, and memories evoked by, my lunch I would have scoffed. But why would I have been so dismissive? Probably because I was scared. Scared to try new things, scared of looking daft, scared of not doing it 'right'.

I've realised that I turned my nose up at activities not because they weren't fun, but because I was nervous about doing them. That nervousness has lifted and I feel I'm so much more positive and willing to open myself up; I'm willing to try and prepared to fail, but also to make sure I don't let that hinder my enjoyment.

Now I had no choice but to throw myself in and say yes if I wanted to have a life; I had to be more creative and willing to give things a chance otherwise I'd have sat at home for a year.

It was with that mindset that I agreed to get involved in a play Trina, an avid amateur dramatics enthusiast, directed. I definitely didn't get up on stage for her production of *Alice in Wonderland* (retitled *Alice in Londonland*, it was about a twenty-something Alice trying to make it in the Big Smoke), but I helped behind the scenes with lighting and rehearsals and Trina and her co-director Kim even let me have input on the storyline.

Despite my preconceptions about am-dram societies, I had an enormous amount of fun and the play was a huge success. Not only that, but I found a new way to spend time with a friend, immersing myself in her world and seeing a different, very inspirational, side to her.

EMBRACING THE CHANGES

When it came to getting stuck in to the challenge of free nights out and weekends spending no money, my husband, family and friends really stepped up to the plate, and I'm very grateful to them.

In fact, many commented to me privately that they could do with saving a few quid themselves so weren't averse to a night out where their wallet could stay firmly in their pocket. Those people would never have come to me and said 'I'm a bit skint, let's do something that's cheap.' I suppose it's all part of keeping up with the Joneses and not wanting to feel left out, a feeling I can definitely relate to.

With everyone on board, it was time to have some money-saving fun. When I started to look around I realised just how many free events were out there and it put into perspective not only how much money I was spending before, but just how predictable my nights out had become.

Why hadn't we bothered doing all this stuff before? Here's a snapshot of just what I got up to during my no spend year:

Theatre trips

I wasn't the biggest fan of theatre, but in the spirit of trying out new things, I got myself a free ticket, via a fellow frugalist @LondonersLondon to see a play called *The Encounter*, the real-life tale of a *National Geographic* photographer who goes missing in the Amazon. The play used 'binaural' technology, meaning the audience wears headphones and the actors are heard in 360-degree sound.

The ticket would have cost between £32 and £42 but I saw the play for free because I agreed to be part of a scientific experiment testing whether people have group reactions. They wired us up to brainwave monitors, which made everyone look like they were on the *Starship Enterprise*, and we got on with watching the play.

It was a bizarre event but the play was so great that I totally forgot someone was looking at my brain as I watched it. I have no idea of the outcome of the experiment but I was grateful to be a part of it.

Of course, the opportunity to be part of a theatre experiment doesn't come along every day, but there are ways to see expensive theatre productions on the cheap. You can get cheap tickets for fringe productions, or queue for last-minute or on-the-day tickets for bigger shows; but if you don't have the spare time to go and queue up there are still ways and means. I haven't used these clubs myself, because you either have to pay a nominal fee to join or you have to pay an administration fee for the complimentary tickets, but others I have told about these sites have used them to great effect.

The Audience Club, My Box Office and The Theatre Club offer tickets for big plays and dance productions for a nominal fee of between £3 and £5 or a donation to their charity of choice. The catch? Well, in order to claim a ticket you *have* to go to the show because they need to get bums on seats and empty theatres look bad (especially on press nights with theatre critics there).

Other than that, you'll probably have to be a bit flexible and see a show on a weeknight rather than a weekend. But if you're going to see a musical for £5 rather than £35, who's complaining?

Comedy nights

Everyone loves a good chuckle now and again and I used to enjoy live stand-up pre-challenge, often shelling out to see big name comedians. Problem is, those tickets cost a bomb.

If you want to see some stand-up then you have to be prepared to sit through some – how do I put this politely? – less seasoned comedians. Open mic nights are a chance to see up-and-coming comedians, and if you're lucky pros trying out new material.

I frequented Angel Comedy in North London, which is on every night of the week and hosts around ten comedians who all do a short set. It was free, except the organisers ask you to contribute £10, or whatever you think it's worth, at the end.

It was quite embarrassing walking past the organisers, who do a great job, at the end of the night and not putting anything into the bucket, and I was worried I'd be pulled up for not giving any money (I wasn't). So although it technically is free, it's really more of a pay-what-you-can night and you have to be able to handle the guilt over contributing nothing (which personally I found quite difficult). I'd consider £10 for an evening at Angel Comedy a bargain though, as you get a lot of laughs for a far cheaper price than at a big show.

The one time I definitely didn't feel guilty about my free comedy was when I got my hands on tickets for well-known comedian Bridget Christie.

Comedians don't just do stand-up shows; quite often they record live DVDs and that's exactly what Bridget Christie was doing. To do that, they need an audience and I bagged my tickets through SRO Audiences, which provides audiences for comedians, panel shows and quiz shows.

Don't expect the evening to be a completely perfect set – the reason you get a free ticket is because you might have to listen to the same joke a few times as they film from different angles or play with the sound.

It's a good way to see big names for nothing, though, and for seeing what goes on behind the scenes at your favourite TV shows. Just make sure you book in advance and keep your fingers crossed that you get a ticket.

Film screenings

I've always felt that the cinema is a bit of a rip-off: £15 for a ticket to see *Iron Man*? I'll wait until it's on telly, thanks. It's one cost I always baulked at and for that reason I didn't actually go to the cinema that much.

I've probably been to more film screenings during my year of not spending than I did the previous year. Granted, I haven't been to see blockbuster, big name movies but that doesn't mean it's not been enjoyable. Most of the tickets I've found have been through the events website Eventbrite, which allows you to search for free events and by type, such as film screenings, plays or classes. It's a constant source of entertainment and you definitely see things you wouldn't have otherwise.

When it comes to films I've had to take what was on offer. Most of the time that has been documentaries, all of them interesting – the best being *The Divide*, about the gap between rich and poor and the role of consumerism in our society. Of course I liked that one! And the bonus of free popcorn and a glass of wine didn't hurt.

And in lieu of a holiday abroad, I went on a 3D journey through America's Yellowstone and Yosemite national parks, courtesy of an American tourism drive.

Just because I personally haven't managed to get my hands on any tickets for big screenings doesn't mean they're not out there. The free-to-join website Free Movies UK has a forum where members post links to free films, and although there are only a few posts up at any one time, I have seen *Blair Witch* and *Captain Fantastic* tickets up for grabs.

Just as with the cheap theatre tickets, the promoters of the films are hoping to fill seats at screenings, and they hope that you'll tell your mates what a good film it was so sales will be boosted via word of mouth.

I'm still happy to wait for big films to make it to DVD, but it's good to have found a source of free films that I probably would never have heard of otherwise.

Museum outings

Living in London, I am spoilt for choice when it comes to museums as many of them are free – however, I hadn't set foot in a lot of them in a very long time, some of them since I was at school.

The past year has given me the opportunity and the time to revisit all the old haunts and I found them as engrossing as ever. Why I didn't come back sooner is anybody's guess, but I suppose few people ask their mates if they want to spend Friday night in the Science Museum and even fewer mates would agree to it.

The big museums, I'm guessing you'll have heard of: the British Museum, Science Museum, Natural History Museum, the V&A, National Maritime Museum, Museum of London and the Imperial War Museum. These are all free, which truly makes them national treasures for both Londoners and visitors to the capital – who could ever be bored?

And when you've exhausted those (although that may take a while) there are lots of smaller museums that I think are worth a mention.

A bit creepy, but nonetheless fascinating, are the deformed skeletons and creatures in jars at the Hunterian Museum, and similarly odd is the Wellcome Collection, which is home to Napoleon's toothbrush! The latter has fantastic exhibitions, both permanent and temporary, and describes itself as a place for the 'incurably curious', which is a spot-on description.

For those in search of even more curios (can you see a theme here?), Sir John Soane's Museum is full of them; packed to the rafters in fact. The tour around the house is a bit spooky and even spookier if done by candlelight.

There are fabulous resources right on my doorstep, so there's no reason for me to ever be bored in London – although admittedly most of the museums are a fair trek from my house, which put a dampener on some of the visits because I had to travel to them all by bicycle.

Revisiting these places – or, for a lot of them, going for the first time – has made me appreciate where I live a lot more. I realised I was taking a lot of what London had to offer for granted. I won't make that mistake again.

Free museums aren't only available in London – most major cities have free days out to enjoy. Manchester has the Imperial War Museum North and the Museum of Science and Industry, while Bristol has the Georgian House Museum.

Leeds has its own museum of the weird in the form of Leeds City Museum, which is home to a collection of beetles and mummies. Further north, Edinburgh has a wealth of free days out, including to the National Museum of Scotland and St Giles' Cathedral.

There's something to do in every city and you're only ever a few mouse clicks away from finding a free day out with some online research.

Gallery tours

As with museums, London is awash with galleries offering you a peek at famous paintings, photographs and sculptures for absolutely nothing.

I don't know much about art but I know that I love getting lost in the expansive galleries dotted around London.

The big galleries attract the big names and if you're interested in seeing paintings by the masters then you can't go wrong with the National Portrait Gallery, Tate Modern, Tate Britain and the Royal Academy of Arts.

Every major city has its own art galleries and the Yorkshire Sculpture Triangle can provide you with days of entertainment, taking you from the Henry Moore Institute and Leeds Art Gallery to the Hepworth in Wakefield and the Yorkshire Sculpture Park in West Bretton.

I enjoyed mixing up the big traditional, established galleries with modern galleries like the Whitechapel and White Cube galleries, plus the smaller unknown galleries tucked away in warehouses and down dimly lit alleyways.

This is why I enjoyed First Thursdays so much. As the name suggests, on the first Thursday of every month galleries across East London have special late-night openings. On offer could be anything from sculpture to photography to a graphics exhibition; part of the fun is that you never know what you're going to find. (As I've said, I'm no art critic so I have to say that for me, the best bit about First Thursdays is that a few of the galleries offer guests free wine and nibbles!)

Alternative arty trips are available for those who want to go off the beaten path in other parts of the country, such as the Banksy walking tour in Bristol; and the Bluecoat in Liverpool is home to new art from contemporary artists, including dance and live art.

Of course, I haven't ridden my bike to all of the places outside of London, I'm not that bonkers, but the next time I'm in any of these places I'm planning on hitting all of the free attractions.

Lectures

Rather than losing brain cells through boozing, this year I've tried to expand my mind just a tiny bit and what better way to do that than through free lectures?

The daddy of the free lecture circuit is the London School of Economics, which has talks on pretty much every weekday on anything from the role of prisons and Norwegian economics to Shakespeare (I didn't say that all the topics were exciting!). You can usually find something to suit your tastes.

When it came to lectures my taste boiled down to three things: consumerism, cycling and travelling.

The nights spent listening to people talk about how consumerism works, the countries they've seen and the cycling they do were both educational and inspiring, mostly making me want to get out on my bike and go on holiday (which admittedly was a bit frustrating at times).

It's incredible that there is so much free education available and so many people willing to share their knowledge. If you're willing to listen and learn, there is an endless stream of people ready to teach you.

Sporting events

All right, so I didn't go to Wimbledon or to any Premier League football matches but I did get to see some sport and, you guessed it, it was cycling.

Cycling is one of the most democratic of sports, which is one reason I love it so much. To see brilliant cyclists you don't have to shell out hundreds of pounds for a season ticket or queue for hours to see them. There are a huge number of bike races that happen on the road and are free for anyone to watch.

This is certainly true in London, which hosts the Prudential RideLondon–Surrey Classic. I actually got the chance to ride the route the pros take as one of 27,000 people who took part in the 100-mile sportive and raise some money for mental health charity Mind in the process.

Then September brought the Tour of Britain to London for a day, in case you hadn't had your fill of sport over the Olympic summer of 2016.

It's not just the big races that London plays host to; there are smaller races such as the Nocturne, which takes place in the evening and sees both professional and semi-pro teams race around the City of London at phenomenal speeds as the sun goes down.

While the big races bring the thrill of famous names and unfathomable speeds, there are smaller amateur and semi-pro races throughout the year that are impressive in a different way

– the people who take part compete at a high level while holding down normal jobs. I'm impressed at how they manage it.

There are fantastic opportunities to watch cycle races at Redbridge Cycle Centre, which is home to the Hoggenberg – a short, sharp climb that makes up part of the race circuit. There's nothing better than taking a picnic down to watch some grass-roots cycling on a sunny day – even if I had to cycle out to Essex to enjoy it.

Gigs

Listening to live music is a real treat, but tickets for a big name band on tour can cost a small fortune. Whether to splash the cash on a Take That reunion tour wasn't a dilemma I had during the no spend year, but I did miss out on some gigs I would love to have gone to.

Instead, I saw lots of new bands courtesy of my local pub, which has bands playing for free five nights a week. It's a fantastic place to hear some great music, and some not so great music, depending on the night. The only catch was I had to sit with my tap water while everyone around me drank their pints.

Not only is it a bit annoying to be surrounded by people who are a bit drunk – you inevitably find more things funny and don't mind repetitive stories when you're pissed – but I also felt really bad for enjoying the music the pub puts on while not contributing anything. My local doesn't put on free music out of the goodness of its heart; the owners want people to come and listen and spend money so that they can *keep* putting free gigs on. By ordering my tap water I wasn't really keeping my end of the bargain and it did make me feel a bit awkward.

If you do want to see well-known musicians play for free then volunteering at festivals is definitely the way to go. Due to diary clashes I didn't manage to fit in any festivals this year, but lots of people recommended volunteering through Oxfam, which supplies stewards and hosts festival shops at festivals up and down the country.

Seeing live music for free and helping out a charity has surely got to be the best of both worlds.

Quirky London

It's not always possible to plan a specific night out when you have no money to spend; you're limited by what's going on for free that night, rather than being able to spend some money to partake in an event. That's why I spent quite a lot of time exploring.

An aimless wander around London was a good way to kill time if I had nothing to do and, in doing this, I stumbled upon interesting things and places that had formerly passed me by. For instance, although I'd previously paid to visit exhibitions in the Barbican I had never entered the conservatory – in fact I didn't know it existed.

It's a beautiful free space festooned with vines and awash with brightly coloured tropical flowers, plus a whole room dedicated to the humble cactus. So many people I've taken had no clue it was there either.

The same goes for London's secret gardens, hidden in walkways between buildings or round the backs of churches – I've now seen areas that I used to go to every week in a totally different light. Mostly it's about keeping your eyes open (and, for me, my head out of my phone) and taking a couple of minutes to detour and see whether there's anything interesting hidden around a corner.

Before I wouldn't have bothered. I rushed from one place to the next, only thinking about where I had to be, not about the places I was passing on the way there. If you've got nothing to do, you don't have anywhere to be then the journey becomes the event.

Boozing

I'm sure that, by now, you've realised I used to spend a lot of time in the pub, but just because I couldn't buy pints any more didn't mean I wanted to spend the year teetotal. I managed to find some ingenious ways to earn some drinks, proving that you don't need a budget to go boozing.

This included free wine-tasting, bizarrely (and maybe a bit irresponsibly) set up in the Look Mum No Hands bicycle café! The South African Wine Company had sponsored a cycle team and wanted to raise their profile in the UK: cue a free, and extremely generous, wine-tasting. Not only did I get some wine out of it, but I bagged myself some free socks as a prize during the event. Result.

Oddly enough, I got myself a place on a beer-cycling tour around London's breweries (what is it with booze and bikes?!). Cycling canals while beer-tasting sounds like a recipe for disaster but thankfully no one veered into the water and I learned a lot about the brewing process, as well as tasting some rather trendy craft beers. The event was organised by Ever Thought of Trying and they usually charge £10 for it but this tour was free as part of London Beer City. Another boozy result!

However, the beer and the wine-tasting pale in comparison to the pint-guzzling I managed to do by volunteering for craft brewer Beavertown's fourth birthday, which it celebrated with a beer festival. The Tottenham-based brewer, which is walking distance from my house, needed staff to volunteer behind the many bars in exchange for some beers on the day and a goody bag of, yep, more beer and a little card entitling you to a total of eight free drinks.

The day was manic and freezing cold but so much fun. There was fantastic camaraderie among the volunteers and I really appreciated my drinks on my subsequent visits to the brewer's bar to redeem my free beer.

I think you'll agree that my fears about turning into a hermit, sitting alone at home for a year, were completely unfounded. It's been a jam-packed year and I haven't spent a penny.

Date nights

There is one person who has probably had to suffer through my challenge almost as much as me: my husband Frank.

Whether it was bike rides in the countryside, wine-tasting, lectures, gigs, galleries – you name it, he's been at my side. It's not easy being the spouse of a person who isn't spending any money and there are plenty of festivals and holidays that Frank has enjoyed this year that I obviously haven't been part of.

Even though he got on with his life away from me, he was restricted by my restrictions – there were no more cosy meals out or trips to the cinema to look forward to. How would we spend our date nights now?

Well, we found something to do that was a lot more fun than a boring meal out, although it is slightly random and maybe not for everyone. We spent our date nights crashing art gallery openings. Told you it was random.

There are tonnes of these all over London, showcasing new artists and exhibitions. Even though I describe it as crashing, technically you're not discouraged from going in, although it can be quite intimidating to bypass the security guard and enter a gallery space with lots of people looking thoughtfully at the paintings and sculptures. Lots of times it was obvious we were there for the free booze and nibbles, but you learn not to act too self-conscious and pretend that you're there to add to your art collection!

It sounds like a silly thing to do but we have such a laugh doing it; it's far more fun than a bog-standard dinner out.

I was discussing eating out with a friend of mine who, along with his partner, eats out around three times a week. After discussing why he spends so much time and money on restaurants, he came to the conclusion it wasn't because he was a foodie but because it's the only time he gets to see his other half without any distraction. The meals out represented quality time spent with the woman he loves and that's what was important to him.

It was interesting to listen to him work through why he spent such a large sum on restaurants; I genuinely think that he hadn't thought about it before. It's part of the problem with today's jam-packed lifestyle; we feel like we have to not just buy items that make our lives more convenient but also buy time with the people we care about.

Spending time with people you love and really talking – and more importantly listening – to them doesn't have to be a precursor to spending money. We're told that time is money, but it doesn't have to be – if you're with the people you love then time doesn't have to cost a thing.

It's all very well for me to say that I was fine with hanging out with my husband and my friends doing free stuff, but what did they think? Well, I asked them and here, in their own words, is what Frank and my dear friend Rowan thought of my challenge.

The husband: Frank

When Michelle told me about her plan for a no spend year I thought she was brave, but mainly insane.

I wasn't convinced she had thought through the impact of such a massive challenge not just on her own life but on others around her. My concerns were mainly based around what we would lose from our lives and how our relationship would be impacted by Michelle living in such a drastic way. I was fearful that she would become a hermit as she would be living outside of everyday social life.

Would it mean my life would be restricted too and I wouldn't see our friends as much? I started to get a bad case of FOMO (fear of missing out).

With no budget for going out I was sure that we'd miss

out on doing the things we used to enjoy and that I'd become frustrated with it all, and that as a consequence I'd become frustrated by Michelle too. You can tell from this how nervous I was, but it was important to Michelle and so I was supportive of her and, even though I thought she was a bit mad, I was proud too.

To show my support I joined in with the grocery part of the challenge, but there was no way I was going to go the whole hog and give up spending! Getting into the swing of the grocery part of the challenge was hard enough – everything had to be planned and prepared for, and that part of my life did feel like a bit of a chore.

But as I got used to living with a no spender, my fears about losing out on time with Michelle, or a lack of spontaneity, subsided. The things I missed at first, like going out for dinner together, were replaced by new experiences and finding things to do together that we probably would never have done previously.

There was an excitement and freshness to our lives as we ventured into the unknown together; visiting new places, meeting new people and sleeping under the stars.

I didn't think I'd say this but our relationship has changed for the better. We've shared unique experiences and are closer than ever. It's not an outcome I expected – I assumed I'd be crossing off the days until Michelle could spend money again.

The challenge has shaken us both out of the mundane and given us a new sense of adventure, and you certainly can't buy that feeling.

The friend: Rowan

We were at a restaurant having dinner to celebrate Michelle's birthday when she dropped the bombshell.

'I've, er, got some news,' she somewhat sheepishly revealed. Promoted? Pregnant? I don't think I could have ever anticipated what she was about to say next. 'I'm not going to spend any money for a whole year.' This was a real forks-down-and-glass-up moment. 'What?!' I'm sure I could feel my debit card grimacing in my pocket.

This news, of course, became the hot topic of conversation among our friends that evening and for many more to come. Everyone opined, because we all, to varying degrees, spend money. Why would she do this? Could I do it? What's the point?

At first I had mixed emotions: pride in Michelle for taking on such a challenge, but also concern that it might impact on our time together.

Of course, there were occasions that were frustrating for Michelle; she was unable to join us on a girls' holiday in the summer and she couldn't spontaneously hop on a bus to travel across London for a quick post-work pint. But, importantly, what didn't change was the quality of the time we shared as friends.

I was quickly reminded of something I learned fifteen years ago when Michelle and I were skint students: you definitely don't need money to have a good time with her. During Michelle's no spend year we actually enjoyed new experiences together because of being unable to go for the easy option of heading straight to the pub.

Instead, we sought out activities we wouldn't have tried before. Another boozy night is easily forgotten, but I'll always treasure our hilarious and eye-opening night at a women's 'sacred circle' in East London, where we were given our own 'power animals'. This resulted in Michelle spending an hour on her hands and knees 'becoming' a wild boar, while I did my best hawk impression. It was priceless in every sense.

I also enjoyed our fun (and totally free!) Saturday morning bike rides in the park, where Michelle kindly taught me how to use my gears properly, and a surprise sleepover that she hosted at her home for our friend's thirtieth birthday. With other friends, she's enjoyed free art galleries and museums, cycling trips and yoga sessions. She's thrown herself into voluntary work and even helped one friend with her fringe theatre production.

Through Michelle, I've been reminded that generosity isn't always about buying family and friends expensive gifts or treating them to a round of drinks, but about giving them your time.

Michelle's reaction to Black Friday and her no spend year also made me think about my own consumerism. Like many of us, I'm guilty of frittering money on rounds of drinks, lunch from Pret, taxis and clothes, often spending money for convenience.

While I wouldn't be brave enough to try a year of no spending, Michelle's challenge has definitely made me more mindful of what I do spend my hard-earned cash on. Do I really need it and, if not, why do I think buying it will make me happier? Michelle hasn't bought anything apart from essential food for a year, and from the sixteen years I've known her, it seems to have been one of her most content and confident ones.

I must be honest, though – I can't wait to go on a big night out with her now the year's up. And with all the money she's saved, the drinks are on her!

I've got a brilliant support network of friends and family, I think you'll agree, and they've all made this year much easier for me by joining in the spirit of the challenge. This doesn't mean it was all plain sailing.

I've missed countless dinners, events, and nights out and each one made me feel a little bit miserable; the only solution I had was to arrange an alternative night for free.

And I think that's the real kicker – not only did I have to constantly arrange nights out, but I had to arrange them to the Nth degree; finding a free event in the first place, which means trawling websites and Twitter, getting people to check their diaries, check how far I'd have to cycle to get to a place, and whether I'd be likely to encounter rain on the way there or back.

The restrictions around what I could do meant impromptu nights were difficult for me, those lovely summer evenings when all your mates are miraculously free after work and you can go to a beer garden. Even if I was free to go, the 'impromptu' bit of the night was dampened by the fact I'd have to cycle and sweat my way to meet them – sometimes I just couldn't face it.

And if I did go to my hypothetical beer garden meet-up, I wouldn't be able to drink. Although friends like Rowan did now and again buy me pints, I generally asked them not to because the challenge wasn't 'a year of getting your mates to pay for your drinks'.

As I've said, this meant I sat around a lot drinking water and watching people get pissed and hearing them repeat the same story three times. Not the best way to spend your evenings but the least I could do when my friends were embracing my bonkers year.

Overall, the good that came from changing the way I socialised far outweighed the bad. The number of new places I've been to, the people I've met, the things I've seen, make up for feeling a bit left out or bored.

I would never have had the impetus to step out of my social comfort zone if I had kept on spending money like I had been.

I'm more willing to say 'yes' to events – a simple word that I don't think I used often enough before, because I was happy doing what I'd always done. The irony of the challenge has been that despite having no money to go out, I've done more, not less – budget isn't a hindrance to a fulfilling social life, your attitude is.

HAVE FUN FOR FREE

You don't have to splash the cash to have fun. With a bit of forward planning you can find free events or at least cut the cost of socialising.

1. Don't be embarrassed

One problem people have with cutting the cost of going out is that they don't want to look mean in front of their mates but the chances are they'd be happy to save a few pounds too. Most people love a bargain, so don't feel embarrassed about suggesting cheaper alternatives when organising plans with friends.

2. The flexible friend

Forget your flexible friend the credit card, *you* have to become the flexible friend! In order to grab a bargain you have to be prepared to go out on weeknights as well as at weekends and to be open about what you will do. By being flexible I was able to, for example, snap up the tickets for Bridget Christie at the last minute that I mentioned earlier.

By keeping your mind and your diary open you'll be better placed to make the most of what comes your way – although be prepared to do some stuff on your own as not everyone may be as willing to be as flexible.

3. Get out and about

Nature is free and when the sun is shining there's no excuse to be bored. Arranging with a friend to take a sandwich to a local park is just as much fun as spending £20 in the pub. You still get to spend time with the people you love, chat to them and have a laugh – and you'll save yourself some money and get some Vitamin D in the process.

If you can combine the trip out with some exercise then even better – it saves on the gym membership!

4. A team effort

I've spoken a lot about being organised and it is key when you want to have a free or cheap night out. We all pay for convenience but if you put the effort into organising free nights out in advance it pays dividends.

Make a deal with friends that you'll have a free night out once a week, or fortnight, or month, and each take turns in organising it so it doesn't fall to the same people over and over again. My friends really jumped on the 'free stuff' band-wagon and although it was slow going at first, they got right into the spirit and were eventually finding free events all over the place.

5. Let me entertain you

You don't have to leave the house to have a good time, and when the weather is rubbish you may not want to leave the house anyway. Entertaining at home doesn't have to cost the earth, and a meal at home is likely to be far cheaper than paying for one in a restaurant.

If you're not a whiz in the kitchen then how about hosting a cocktail party (with everyone contributing a bottle of some-thing), or a film night? Even a night mucking around playing board games or charades can be fun if you've got your best friends with you.

6. Keep your eyes peeled

If you want to find out about free and cheap events then you need to be signed up to the websites that let you know what's on. The Eventbrite website is an amazing resource and lets you search events based on topic, the type of event such as film screening or lectures, the location and price.

Similar to Eventbrite is Billetto, although it seems to be slightly more focused on food events. One person told me they use the latter to find soft launches for new restaurants, where new eateries open with a set menu for a discounted price to test their waiting staff and kitchens. Of course, I haven't actually tried any soft launches because you have to pay for those!

7. Never pay full price

If you want to save money, then don't pay full price. If you know you're going out to eat with your other half, pick your restaurant based on what voucher codes you can get your hands on. There are loads of vouchers out there offering 2-for-1 and discounted dinners; all it takes is a quick Internet search.

The same goes for cinema tickets; instead of going to a multiplex, go to a local, smaller cinema – they are more likely to offer discounted off-peak tickets, although the film choice is also likely to be more limited. Similarly, the matinee showing of a theatre production is generally cheaper than an evening show.

In short: search for and use your voucher codes with pride.

8. Learn something

Gossip and laughs tend to make up most nights out, for me and my friends anyway, and although I agree this is a lovely way to spend time with friends it can be just as rewarding learning something together.

A museum tour, lecture or even a free workshop can still bring laughs (if you end up in a women's sacred circle!) but you get to expand your mind at the same time. I can't really think of a time pre-challenge when my friends and I did something 'educational', but now we're all open to the idea of talks and classes as a different way to spend time with one another. You can always debate the lecture afterwards in the pub too!

9. Special events
Whatever you're into, there's usually a day or a week that celebrates it – whether that's Bike Week, National Gardening Week or National Toast Day (yes, it's a thing) – and there are bound to be loads of events, exhibitions and talks organised around it, many of them for free.

If you're mad about yoga for example, September plays host to National Yoga Month, with free classes and yoga-related events taking place up and down the country.

The aim of these awareness days is to promote whatever sport or hobby they are about, so you're bound to find something free to do as they try to entice people in.

10. Make use of public spaces
Ever spent money in a café because you wanted to use the free Wi-Fi and sit down for an hour? I have. Dropping a fiver just so I could rest my legs and check my emails without running down my phone data.

You don't have to – plenty of public spaces have free Wi-Fi. I've mentioned the Barbican and Royal Festival Hall, which have the added bonus of offering some free exhibitions (Barbican) and some free concerts (Royal Festival Hall), so when you go in to take your breather you could also enjoy a performance.

And a top tip for when you're in London – free public amphitheatre The Scoop offers a range of free events from plays to exercise classes. Just turn up and join in the fun.

HOW DO YOU RATE YOURSELF?

Credit ratings are a funny old thing. When you're applying for a loan they can seem the stuff of nightmares, but you shouldn't be scared of your rating.

You've probably got a vague idea of whether you have a good or a bad rating depending on how you manage your money.

But the thing is, credit ratings aren't like Santa's naughty and nice list. In fact, there is no definitive 'list' of who banks should and shouldn't lend to.

All lenders have their own ratings criteria that they will judge you against if you apply to take out a mortgage, personal loan or credit card. Some lenders are stricter than others and some put more weight on certain factors.

If one bank won't lend to you that doesn't mean that others automatically won't.

However, if you've missed loads of credit card and phone bill repayments in the past then chances are you're not a good bet for a loan and will likely be rejected.

Having been bad with money in the past isn't the only thing that can affect your credit rating with banks.

A credit rating is a bank's way of trying to predict how reliable you will be in paying back any money it lends you. If you haven't borrowed any money in the past, though, it's going to have a hard job predicting that – people with limited credit history are known in the industry as 'thin files'.

This is why people will often say it's good to take out a credit card. Credit cards can help you build up a good credit rating for when you need a large loan like a mortgage, as long as you pay the balance off swiftly.

If you're unsure about how you rate and want to know more you can always use a credit rating agency; they typically offer a basic service for free.

These agencies hold a huge amount of data about individuals and help lenders decide whether or not you are a good bet.

They compile data from the electoral roll, details of other times you've applied for credit and previous credit checks done on you, and the number of bank accounts, loans and credit cards you already have. They also take information from the courts to track county court judgements and bankruptcies against your name.

Banks fill in the gaps by sharing information – including your income – with one another to give a more rounded picture of your finances.

The credit rating agencies can build a pretty good picture of where your money comes from and how you allocate it, so you need to ensure your finances are in order.

How to make sure your credit rating is in tip-top condition:

1. Make sure you are on the electoral roll. This proves you exist and if you're not on the register it's unlikely you'll get any credit.
2. Before making any big loan applications, check your score with one of the agencies. This will flag up any black marks that may have been added to your record by mistake that will hinder your application. Clear up any mistakes before applying for credit; every time you apply and are turned down, it will appear as a footprint on your file.
3. If your finances are linked to another person, such as your partner or spouse, make sure their credit score doesn't hold you back. Get them to check their credit rating too.
4. Don't make too many applications. Footprints stay on your file for twelve months and too many, or lots in a short space of time, will look bad.
5. Don't skip repayments. It may seem obvious but it's worth saying: the best way to a good credit score is by being good with credit and making sure you don't miss credit card, electricity and phone bills.

GETTING ON THE PROPERTY LADDER

Pensions and investments are those kind of financial topics that people aren't interested in, are scared of, or just simply hadn't given a second thought to.

But there is one financial topic that people are always interested in: property.

People may not know how much is in their pension but you can bet they'll know how much their house is worth (and how much their neighbour's house is worth for that matter!).

Getting a mortgage is not just a financial milestone but a life milestone, and while it's exciting to buy your first property it's also a huge responsibility.

If you've saved the deposit to buy a place then chances are you've already made a series of good financial decisions such as prioritising your spending, maybe cutting back in order to save more, and working out where to put your money in order to get the best savings rate.

So the first thing is not to undo all your good work by going to your bank and asking for a mortgage. Just because you've had your current account with the same bank for ten years doesn't mean they'll give you the best mortgage deal.

Instead, to get the best mortgage use an independent mortgage broker who will have access to special mortgage rates and be able to advise you on the best one for your personal circumstances.

Although a broker is invaluable for helping you with the details, it's worth knowing about the basics of mortgages before you try to get one.

Strict rules

Getting a mortgage these days isn't as easy as it was pre-financial crisis, when huge loans were given out willy-nilly.

Banks now have to abide by strict lending rules to ensure they're not giving a loan to someone who can't afford it. The lender will want to see three months, possibly more, of bank statements, plus evidence of your income, and they will ask lots of questions about your lifestyle, which may seem very personal: they might ask, for example, whether you have a child on the way, so they can factor childcare and maternity or paternity leave into their lending equation.

If you are self-employed then you're going to have to jump through even more hoops. Lenders typically won't lend to someone with less than two years of business accounts and most prefer three years' worth.

And even when you are accepted, you probably won't be able to borrow as much money as you would if you earned the same salary as an employed person working for a company.

There are lots of factors a lender will consider before they confirm how much you can borrow; just be honest with your mortgage broker about your finances because the strict lending criteria are there to protect you as well as the bank. You don't want to borrow more than you can manage.

The basics of mortgages

There are two main types of mortgages.

Fixed versus trackers

The first is a fixed mortgage that has a set interest rate attached to it. With this type of mortgage you pay a set amount every month for as long as the deal lasts. This can be anywhere from two years to ten years.

The second is a tracker mortgage, where the interest rate fluctuates depending on the base rate set by the Bank of England, which is currently 0.25%.

If for example the tracker rate on offer was base rate+1% then your interest rate would be 1.25% (0.25% + 1%).

Tracker rates mean your mortgage payments could go up or down depending on whether the base rate goes up or down.

Rates

At the time of writing, mortgage rates have been low for a long time thanks to a base rate that sat at a historic low of 0.5% for nearly eight years, and then was cut further to 0.25% post-Brexit. Economists on the Bank of England's monetary policy committee (MPC) decide whether the base rate should go up or not and it has a knock-on effect on the cost of lending.

When the base rate is low, it's good for borrowers because mortgage rates are low and mortgage repayments are cheaper. However, they can go up, meaning that mortgage rates and repayments would become more expensive.

When calculating how much you can afford to borrow, the lenders won't base affordability on current low mortgage rates but on a scenario where you have to pay a higher mortgage rate in future, with some testing at rates as high as 7%.

The rate you receive will also depend on how much of a deposit you put down and is known as the loan-to-value (LTV) ratio. For example, if you put down a 10% deposit your LTV will be 90%; the lower the LTV the cheaper the mortgage.

Fees

Mortgages cost money. It's not just the interest paid back on the loan; you may also have to pay a fee for taking out the mortgage. The fees vary from zero to over £2,000 depending on the deal.

The better the mortgage rate the higher the fee is likely to be.

Lenders will offer to roll your mortgage fee into the loan, meaning you will pay interest on the money that you borrow to pay the fee; if you can afford to pay the fee up front then do.

Term

The mortgage term is how long you have to pay back your loan. Traditionally, people took out mortgages for twenty-five years but as we are all living and working longer and property is becoming more expensive, loans of thirty and thirty-five years are becoming more common.

The longer the term the cheaper your monthly payments will be as the loan is stretched over a longer period.

Note that even though your mortgage will be paid back over many years, the mortgage deal you take – whether fixed or tracker – is not going to be for the whole term. This means you will have to apply for a new deal in future, which may be set at a totally different rate.

Repayments

Your monthly repayments cover both the interest and the capital of the loan.

Let's take the example of a £250,000 property. You put down a 10% deposit (£25,000) so you need a mortgage of £225,000. You get a mortgage rate of 3% to be paid back over thirty years.

Your repayments will be £949 a month.

Of that repayment £387 will go towards paying down the capital (the £225,000) you have borrowed and £562 will go towards paying the interest on the loan.

You can roughly calculate how much of your mortgage payment is going towards interest by using this formula (don't worry, it's not as complex as it seems).

3 (mortgage rate) / 12 (months in a year) x 225,000 (the balance of the mortgage) = 56,250

This means £562 of the £949 you pay each month is just servicing the interest on the loan.

So the remaining £387 (£949 − £562) is paying down the capital. Not much is going towards the actual loan, which is why it takes so long to pay off a mortgage.

Overpayment

Your mortgage company wants you to pay back your loan over the longest time period possible because that way it makes more in interest. But you don't have to play by their rules.

You can overpay your mortgage (pay more than the monthly amount set by the bank). Typically you can overpay 10% of the total outstanding loan each year and some lenders will let you overpay a certain amount each month – often £500 – before you start to incur fees.

By overpaying your mortgage you can chop down the term of your loan and also reduce the total amount of interest you pay on the loan.

As you pay down the loan the percentage of your repayment going towards the capital increases and the amount going towards interest decreases (remember the 'snowball' effect we talked about before?)

Let's go back to our example of the person with a £225,000 mortgage. They are paying £949 a month and just £387 of that is actually paying off the loan; the rest is going towards the interest.

Now imagine our person has overpaid their mortgage and got the balance down to £200,000. They will still be paying monthly repayments of £949 but more of the money will be paying down the loan and less of it will be paying off the interest.

3 (mortgage rate) / 12 (months in a year) x 200,000 (outstanding mortgage) = 50,000

This means £500 of the £949 is going towards the interest.

The remaining £449 (£949 – £500) is going towards the capital.

The more you overpay, the more of your repayment goes towards paying back the loan.

Make sure you inform the bank that you are overpaying and ensure that it takes the money overpaid off the 'capital' of your loan so that the term of the loan decreases. If you don't then your bank may assume you are overpaying to reduce the payments you make each month, but doing this won't reduce the term of your mortgage.

Remortgaging

The length of your mortgage term will be far longer than your mortgage deal, which means that when your deal is up you need to remortgage.

Remortgaging can be a good or a bad thing depending on how the property market has done. If your house has risen in value in the time you've owned it, when you remortgage your LTV will be lower and you could get a better deal (provided mortgage rates haven't gone up in that time).

Alternatively, if house prices have fallen in that time your LTV could stay the same; and in a worst-case scenario you could find yourself in 'negative equity', where your home is worth less than the amount you owe.

There is no way of knowing how much value you will have in your home when you come to remortgage, but remortgaging is better than doing nothing. If you don't remortgage then your mortgage rate will revert to a 'standard variable rate' (SVR), which is typically far higher than mortgage rates on offer.

Basically this is a penalty rate for being too lazy to sort out a remortgage. By letting your mortgage run on to an SVR you'll likely end up paying more each month than you were before – and certainly more than if you shopped around again.

THE
NO
SPEND
YEAR

PEDAL
POWERED
ADVENTURES:
HOLIDAYING
ON THE
CHEAP

Tack, tack, tack, tack, tack, tack, tack, tack. Clunk.

The noise, coming from the back of my bike, didn't sound right. My heart sank; we were 150 miles from home on a cycling holiday. I couldn't afford for my bike to fail on me now.

I glanced back and immediately hit the brakes.

My waterproof jacket that had been strapped to the back of my bike had come loose and was threatening to tangle itself in my back wheel and cogs, the sleeves flailing wildly behind me. It had been a close shave. I felt so relieved.

But as I was packing my jacket back in, I looked at my trainers, which had been strapped to the bike along with my jacket. Only one of them was there.

I was two days into my holiday and already a trainer down. I'd spend the rest of the holiday either in my cycling shoes or barefoot.

If anyone was on the Suffolk coast in August and found a worse-for-wear, white, size 8 plimsoll between Lowestoft and Great Yarmouth, it's mine!

As you will have gathered my bike has been an integral part of the no spend year. I'd go as far to say it was my most important possession (along with all the bits that go with it).

As part of the challenge, I'd set myself a budget of zero

for transport, so I'd have to go everywhere under my own steam.

Lots of people have asked me why I made this bit so difficult for myself as most people would class travel costs as an essential. It is a bit bold, but I cycled most of the time pre-challenge anyway (I'd estimate 60% of my journeys) so why not just do 100%?

I'd done some long bike rides pre-challenge too, with the furthest I'd cycled being 120 miles, so part of me thought that cycling everywhere wouldn't be too much of a stretch from what I did normally. And if I was going to do a crazy challenge, why not go the whole hog?

But hands up, I completely underestimated how demanding cycling, and sometimes walking, everywhere would be.

It has been an exhausting part of the challenge. A rough calculation reveals I've cycled on average 125 miles a week, or 6,500 over the course of the year.

But I've done it and for that I'm really proud of myself. Especially when I weigh up those miles against the amount of money I spent on travel in the previous year.

Keeping in mind that I had already been cycling for around 60% of my journeys in the year before, I still managed to spend £960 on train tickets, the tube, bus fares and taxis. That's a huge sum of money and one that I would never have even guessed at had you asked me.

I didn't quite realise how much my travel was costing me and because I cycled so much already anyway I had figured that I couldn't possibly have been spending more than a few hundred quid in total. Wrong!

Popping down to see my brother or sister near Gatwick Airport costs me £20 return, a daily Travelcard in London is an extortionate £12.10, and a cab ride after one too many pints can be upwards of £25 depending on where I've been. It all added up to a huge sum.

We all have to travel; it's essential for getting to work, meeting our friends, visiting family, buying food, and generally getting out and about. It was a serious consideration when deciding what should and shouldn't be included in my essential costs and there were times that I regretted not giving myself a travel budget.

Working out how to get everywhere under my own steam was difficult and, much like the grocery shopping, it took a lot of organisation.

Every time I planned to go anywhere, I had to work out how long it would take me and factor that into my day, working out where I could lock my bike in a place that would be safe, think about where I would be able to get changed out of (and then later back into) my cycling gear, and ensure I had everything I needed for a puncture.

When you ride a bike, it's not just the bicycle you have to think about and my backpack went everywhere with me (despite the fact the waterproof coating wore off at the beginning of the year, meaning I had to keep everything in plastic bags!).

The contents of my bag included: front and rear lights (rechargeable LED lights so no need for batteries), lock, cable for extra security, tyre levers, spare inner tubes x 2, puncture repair kit – 6 x patches, a mini-pump, a multi-tool, waterproof jacket. And a helmet, of course.

These are things I owned pre-challenge, along with two pairs of cycling shorts, a base layer, some cycling tops and cycle shoes that enable you to clip your shoes into the pedals. I also had half a bottle of bike oil.

My biggest fear was punctures because I had a limited supply of inner tubes and repair patches. Unfortunately my fear became all the more real when the first week brought my first puncture. I was gutted and prayed to the cycling gods that this wasn't a sign of things to come.

Thankfully it wasn't and I had only five punctures over the year so had enough supplies to repair them. Punctures are always annoying but the good news is I can change an inner tube in record time now!

Kindness of strangers

While I was relying on luck when it came to punctures, there was one bike-related problem no amount of luck or praying would change: the fact that my brake pads would wear out. As I didn't stock up on parts pre-challenge, I started my no spend year with brake pads that were fairly well used already. By the end of June I knew they were wearing thin and had to start thinking about how I could get my hands on some pads for free. A number of people have questioned why I didn't just buy some – they're pretty essential to someone who gets around by bike. I do see their point but the aim was to try to get through the year without spending and only a real emergency would justify me breaking my spending ban.

My ban didn't just mean I wouldn't buy anything new, it also meant I wouldn't buy replacements for the items I already own. I haven't replaced anything in the entire year; even when my cycling leggings split I just wore them with shorts underneath (I didn't want to get arrested!) and I didn't replace my lost trainers. If something wore out or got lost, it was tough luck – I just had to make do with what I had left.

That said, trying to find brake pads was hard going and I honestly thought this would be the point I had to put my hand in my pocket until a kind Glaswegian called Bean answered my call on Twitter. I had asked whether anyone would be willing to trade me replacement brake pads for my time, helping them out with whatever jobs or projects they had on. Bean had sent out brake pads the next day and all she wanted in return was for me to 'pay it forward'. What a star.

As I waited for my brake pads to arrive, I got the chance to do as Bean had asked. Cycling home one evening I passed a young woman who was running down the road crying. I stopped to see if I could help and it turned out she had been mugged by two thieves on a moped who had snatched her phone out of her hand. She used my phone to call the police and try to contact her boyfriend. I waited with her until they arrived.

The poor woman had only been in London for a few weeks and, remembering what Bean had said, I decided to find her a new phone. It took me precisely eight minutes from asking on Twitter if anyone had a spare phone to a lovely person offering one up.

They sent it to my house and as I had the woman's boyfriend's contact number I was able to track her down and give her the phone.

I'm not telling you this to brag. I'm telling you because I think it shows that 'paying it forward' works – and that it makes the world a slightly nicer place. If Bean hadn't sent me those brake pads, I would still have stopped to help the mugged woman but would I have gone a step further and found her a phone? Honestly, I don't know.

When the woman asked how she could repay me, I told her what Bean had told me.

The brake pads, as it turned out, got lost in the post so I was back to square one on that front, but even so I felt I had learned a very valuable lesson. Kindness spreads; we just all need to have the opportunity to do a nice thing.

I did eventually get hold of some used brake pads from a bike-mad friend who was selling a load of used parts. He handed over four pads that he didn't need and which wouldn't sell. He's the one who kept me safely on the road rather than whizzing round town on half a brake pad!

I also managed to get two free cleats (the bit of plastic that attaches to cycle shoes so you can clip them into the pedals). Someone was giving away a lightly used pair on a London bike forum and Frank picked them up for me. You know what they say: one man's trash is another woman's treasure. It amazes me what people give away if you spend the time looking.

When you own a bike, it's never completely smooth sailing

and I also had a problem with my gears – I basically couldn't change gears without my chain falling off. After brilliant recommendations for online tutorials I managed to fix the problem, with a bit of help from Frank too.

I'm no expert bike mechanic but I do feel a lot more confident now about looking after my bike. Not only can I get to places under my own steam but I can also fix, at least temporarily, a host of problems. Getting a full bike service after a year of my amateurish tinkering is a must though!

When people asked me what I would buy when the spending ban ended, my first thought was always 'Bicycle', and cycle leggings were top of the list. Strangely, I thought I'd be hankering after new everything, but what I looked forward to purchasing were practical items; keeping me and my bike on the road really has become my priority.

Knowing what can go wrong with a bike and how to (sort of) fix it was also some comfort when I went on holiday. Yes, you can go on holiday when you're not spending anything! But it probably won't be a holiday as you know it

EXPERIMENTS WITH FREE HOLIDAYS

Lots of people assumed I prepared extensively for the challenge, maybe by bulk-buying inner tubes and 365 bottles of wine, but I didn't; I worked with what I already had. The only thing I purchased to help me on the no spend year was two bike-packing bags.

These are bags that strap to your bike frame and handlebars so you can carry supplies on your bike and so travel long distances. We already had a tent, sleeping bags and blow-up mattresses; having the bike-packing bags to carry them in would mean Frank and I would be able to go on a cycle holiday.

I know what you're thinking though: campsites cost money, and I don't have any money to spend. You're right. Campsites do cost money and that's why we didn't stay at any. Instead we went 'wild camping'.

Essentially this means camping anywhere you can find.

It's only permitted in Scotland, where you can camp anywhere, and in some places in England and Wales including Dartmoor. If you do a bit of research you'll find there are loads of people at it and books devoted to it. Some people hedge their bets and camp anywhere, while others get permission from the landowner to camp in a field or woodland.

While I can't under the laws of the land, encourage you to go wild camping, I can say that if you do go, the first rule is to leave no trace (i.e. clean up after yourself) and don't make a nuisance of yourself.

The first wild camping trip we did as a test run was just one night. Inspired by adventurer Alastair Humphreys's micro-adventures, we decided to see if we could have a micro-adventure of our own just an hour from our house.

That's how we ended up cycling ten miles up the canal out of London to a nature reserve on a Saturday night and camping among muntjacs and bats.

After observing the area for an hour to make sure no one was going to wander past, we scarpered into some trees and set up camp.

Sitting out under a canopy of stars listening to the woods settle in for the night, we were hooked. Our next wild camping adventure would be for much longer and take us far further from home.

In fact, it took us on a 370-mile trip through Essex, along the Suffolk and Norfolk coastline.

THE BIG HOLIDAY

I love going on holiday; it's the thing I liked to spend money on the most and I knew it was going to be the thing I missed the most.

Between visiting family in Ireland, an annual girls' holiday, summer holidays and bank holiday city breaks I'd estimate I spent between £2,500 and £3,000 a year travelling to different locations. It's a considerable sum of money, I know, but it was also a considerable number of holidays. Could one UK cycle holiday on zero budget ever really compete?

The answer is yes, but only if you change your mindset about holidaying. Pre-challenge my holidays would follow a similar pattern. I'd check TripAdvisor for the best things to do and nice restaurants to eat in, and make sure we were staying in a nice area. When we got there, we'd tick off the tourist attractions on the list and queue up to visit museums and churches. I'd make sure some relaxation time was booked in, but not too much – you don't want to be a slouch on your holiday and miss out on another monument!

And our big summer holiday would often involve travelling around different areas within a country, meaning the TripAdvisor list would have to be updated for each new town.

None of that matters when you have no money. You can only travel so far for a start – essentially as far as your legs will take you. And when you get to a destination, it doesn't matter which restaurant is the best in town because you can't eat in it. Neither does it matter which museums are top-rated because, unless they're free, you can't visit them anyway.

Although holidaying without a budget brings its own struggles, it did take the pressure off because we couldn't do the normal 'tourist things'. In fact, there's not much to do but relax. I'm not very good at relaxing; I find it hard to sit still and enjoy my surroundings. However, with wild camping enjoying the surroundings is pretty much all you can do.

So let me tell you about our holiday. We planned a rough route that would take us up and down hills and along blustery coastline, then back home, over six days. It would be a lot of cycling but the scenery would be beautiful and I was really looking forward to it. Even the prospect of being on a bike for hours every day (ten hours on one particular day) wasn't putting me off because I was so excited to be having a holiday and a break from work.

Other than planning a route that kept us away from busy roads and having a look on Google Maps to identify possible places to sleep, we couldn't really plan anything. We had to leave the holiday pretty much to chance.

Every time we hit a new village we'd have a wander around, find the local shop, identify a place to pitch our tent and then find a spot with a view where we could have our dinner. When the sun went down we'd pitch our tent for the night. I'd recommend taking a deck of cards or a book!

The next day it starts all over again. If you're going to cycle from place to place, you have to enjoy cycling. I obviously do, so for me and Frank part of the fun was getting to the places we stayed at and stopping at interesting points on the way. And I can say that I'm also much fitter after a week of lugging all my clothes and food along on my bike.

Diary of a Wild Camping Adventure

Dear Diary . . .
Wednesday 10 August
It's our third wedding anniversary and to celebrate we decided to take a holiday!

Well, holiday might be pushing it a bit - it's probably fairer to say we decided to have an adventure.

An adventure that has destroyed me on the first day. So instead of a civilised city break we've sat on our bikes for nine hours and ended up 100 miles from our house, in a Suffolk forest.

It's a long way to go to sleep in some creepy woods and

was made even harder by the fact that we had to carry all our camping gear, clothes and as much food as we could pack in. In total it was probably an extra two and a half to three stone of weight each.

It felt like a long day and I really questioned why we were doing it. I'm sure Frank was questioning why he agreed to even marry me if this was the sort of hare-brained scheme I was coming up with!

I have to admit I have felt guilty today, not only for making him do this but for getting a bit grumpy and snappy throughout the day. It was the ideal way to celebrate an anniversary.

As I'm writing this, we're finally tucked up in the tent with bats flapping overhead and I've never been so grateful to be in a sleeping bag.

I've got a feeling these next few days are going to be more boot camp than relaxing break.

Miles ridden: 100
Money spent: £0: we ate the food we'd brought with us
Holiday feel: 2/10

Thursday 11 August

We must have really needed to sleep last night because we didn't wake up until 9.30 a.m., meaning we got over ten hours' sleep.

We were straight on the bikes and over to Southwold, which is a quaint seaside town.

The weather was a bit overcast and windy so we couldn't go down to the beach, but we ate our remaining pasta looking out over the sea.

After a trip to the pub, where I had my usual pint of tap water, we headed off further up the coast.

It would have been an easy ride if it wasn't for the incident with my missing shoe, which disappeared off the back of my bike!

The fact I lost my shoe did make me laugh. I wonder whether I'd have been this laid-back about it before the challenge? Part of me thinks it would have made me more annoyed but I'm not sure why. Maybe because I know I can't do anything about the shoe – I have no idea where it fell off and I can't buy any new ones, which means I just have to get on with it.

We ended up in a little seaside village for the night. It's picture postcard perfect with brightly coloured houses, a lighthouse and sand dunes on which to camp.

We loaded up at a supermarket earlier in the day, so had the dinner of champions on the beach: houmous, bread, tomatoes, crisps and er . . . tinned potatoes!

It's so peaceful here and so lovely, I'm glad we're relaxing here tomorrow and not going anywhere.

Miles ridden: 57
Money spent: £3.88 in the supermarket and £1.20 on water
Holiday feel: 7/10

Friday 12 August
Today we didn't go anywhere except the beach and it really felt like a holiday. The weather was absolutely glorious and the free factor-50 sunscreen we'd picked up on Olio got put to good use.

As we had to cycle to go anywhere outside of the town (which we didn't want to do) and I couldn't pay to do anything in town (not that there was much to do), we were forced to relax. We couldn't even check our phones because we had no signal. All that was left to do was sit and enjoy the view and enjoy a chilly swim.

I can't remember the last time I did nothing. Even on

holidays before, I would have been packing in the sightseeing and making sure I ticked off the monuments and churches listed on TripAdvisor. Not today. Today was all about doing sod-all and it was the best day.

Miles ridden: 0

Money spent: £5.79 on bread, tomatoes, lots of water (why don't we have water fountains in this country?) and cold baked beans for dinner!

Holiday feel: 10/10

Saturday 13 August

We tried to hang on to yesterday's relaxing vibe by packing up the tent and then falling back to sleep on the beach.

We finally set off at midday and cycled up the Norfolk coast. It was bloody windy and all afternoon we were battered by headwinds and crosswinds. After hours of it, the winds weren't the only thing that were cross.

Although we'd had bread and peanut butter (which we'd brought with us) for breakfast, I was starving. The little towns that we went past had rather unappetising selections of pork pies and sausage rolls, not great for a veggie.

In the end we had some chips from the chip shop. It felt like an amazing treat to buy hot food, not just because I've only eaten cold food on the trip but because that's the first time I've bought food that I've not had to cook myself for the entire challenge. Maybe it was a bit of a cheat but I had to eat.

Fuelled by potato, we made it to a fishing village. What an amazing place. We spent an hour or so looking out over the sea talking about the trip and chatting to a couple, who were caravanning, about wild camping.

We've just pushed our bikes out on to the beach (which was no easy task over sand) and have set up camp behind some beach huts. Sitting outside watching the stars coming out is a fantastic way to spend an evening.

Miles ridden: 51

Money spent: an unhealthy 'breakfast' of crisps and water from the local shop set us back £2.19, then £3.90 on two portions of chips for lunch. We picked up dinner of pitta bread, houmous and tomatoes plus water at the supermarket for £3.10. Total £9.19 for the day.

Holiday feel: 9/10

Sunday 14 August

We got up early today as we had a long cycle ahead of us to get back down to Suffolk. But I didn't care because I knew at the end of the ride we'd have a hot meal and a snuggly bed waiting.

We set off to our friends Lou and Vaughn's, where we'd be staying the night.

It's amazing what fun games you can play to amuse yourself on the road (there's only so many fields you can 'ooh' at). The game mostly consisted of me singing really loudly and badly, so not so much fun for Frank!

When I wasn't belting out 'Come on Eileen', being on the road for ten hours gave me a chance to think. I know that may sound silly but it's not very often we have uninterrupted time to just have a think about our lives or whatever things we're worried about, or try to find solutions to problems. It was nice to get lost inside my little cycle head.

It was even better to arrive at our friends' house. The bed I'm in feels like a cloud and we have bellies full of pasta and wine.

Miles ridden: 86

Money spent: breakfast was leftover bread and peanut butter (we bought three jars with us!) and for lunch we spent £4.50 on pasta, couscous and some rolls. Dinner at our friends' house.

Holiday feel: 7/10

Monday 15 August

We left early again this morning after waving Lou and Vaughn off to work and having some strong coffee.

We set a course for home but we were going to make a detour to another friend's house for lunch.

After battling around hilly old Essex we made it and were greeted by Colette, her little boy and new baby girl. Frank made the most of the paddling pool while we gossiped and I had my first cuddle with the new arrival.

And then we were on the final straight home.

After six days on the road I'm tired but actually a bit sad that our wild camping adventure/bicycle boot camp has come to an end. I've got calloused hands, tan lines that make me look like I'm wearing cycle shorts and an aching back. It was a blast.

Miles ridden: 77

Money spent: breakfast with one friend and lunch with another but we had to buy supplies for dinner on the way home totalling £5.67.

Holiday feel: 9/10

Total miles ridden: 371

Total money spent on food: £30.23

Would I do it again? Definitely!

I don't want to make it sound like it's all jolly hockey sticks though; there are elements of wild camping that are difficult and you have to be prepared for them.

If you're camping in the middle of nowhere you don't have access to showers or toilets. We washed just once during our holiday and, as it was a dip in the sea, I don't know if it even really counts as 'having a wash'! Thankfully seaside villages often have public toilets near the beach, but failing that local pubs were a lifesaver.

Camping in random areas can also be a bit nerve-wracking if you start to hear odd noises, which is bound to happen in the woods. You do get used to them though and I can now easily sleep through the whole night without waking up worrying that I'm going to be the next victim of an axe murderer.

Thanks to the challenge, eating was also a bit of a pain. If you were planning on wild camping you could of course have your dinner in a pub en route, but that wasn't an option for us. Instead we had to rely on local shops and detours out to big supermarkets where we could in order to buy supplies. It wasn't always easy to find ways to eat, especially when we ended up in remote parts of the country, which is why I resorted to eating chips for one meal.

We tried to take as much food as possible but you have to make sure it will keep and that it can provide lots of energy to give you pedal power. I dread to think how much boring bread and peanut butter I ate.

As we don't have a camping stove all our food was cold, which wasn't ideal, and for future wild camping trips I would definitely invest in a little cooker – and maybe some travel board games to help while away the evenings.

I suppose the point is there will definitely be future trips. Although it was slightly knackering, my long-distance camping adventure didn't put me off at all and I'd be happy to do it again (probably with some detours to the pub for dinner next time). I've been given so many cycle holiday tips for both UK and European destinations that it would be a shame to waste them. I'm already trying to decide where to go next.

Wild camping isn't going to float everyone's boat and I'm sure that some people couldn't think of anything worse than wandering into the woods to sleep.

But putting to one side the issues surrounding the kind of holiday we had, our no spend trips have given me so much more than a week off work. They've enabled me to have a spontaneous break and forced me to relax, partly thanks to the lack of phone signal.

Switching off and getting lost in a different part of the country was so exciting, and far less sanitised than the holidays I've taken before. Yes I was smelly from not washing, and yes I was tired from riding my bike, but I felt happy sitting on the sand dunes looking out to sea. I didn't have a care in the world.

Our initial ten-mile journey and one night of wild camping inspired 370 miles of cycling and six nights of beach and forest dwelling, but it has also inspired far more. From now on, if there's an adventure to be had, I'm in and I'm not even going to check TripAdvisor for the best place to eat fish and chips!

TOP TIPS FOR FRUGAL ADVENTURES

Travel is a necessity, and can also be a luxury, but whether you're going to work or want a week away, it doesn't have to cost the earth.

1. Under your own steam

This tip is to be expected from me, I know, but there's a lot to be said for travelling somewhere under your own steam, whether you walk, cycle or maybe kayak . . . There's a real sense of achievement and you save money on costly train fares and cab rides.

You don't have to go far; even choosing to walk into town rather than take the car means you save money on petrol, get some exercise and, you never know, you may spot something interesting on the way.

2. Look after your wheels

Whether it's a bike or a car, you should know the basics of looking after your mode of transport.

Knowing how to change the oil in the car, keep your radiator topped up and your tyres at the right air pressure will help maintain your car and prevent bigger problems, plus costly mechanics' bills, further down the line.

When it comes to bicycles, they're easy to maintain once you know how. Start with learning to change an inner tube (you'd be surprised how many cyclists can't do this) and progress to more complex things like changing brake pads – you'll master it in no time.

3. Walk and learn

After living in London for over a decade I'm still discovering new green spaces and interesting monuments just by walking around.

Having an aimless stroll around an area is the best way to learn about it, whether you're at home or on holiday. You don't always have to rely on guidebooks to tell you about the secrets of a city – try finding them out for yourself.

4. Day-to-day adventures

Getting up, going to work, eating lunch, working some more, going home. It's pretty boring but most of us have to face the daily grind (until we win the lottery).

But there are ways to make it more fun that don't cost loads of money or take loads of time. You can easily have a small adventure by varying your route home from work to walk somewhere pretty you haven't been before, or having your dinner in a park.

Adventures don't have to be consigned to the two weeks of holiday you take a year.

5. Duty-free isn't free

If you are flying somewhere nice for your holidays, avoid the duty-free shopping unless you've done your price match research.

Just because something is VAT-free doesn't mean it's free, and although something has cost you £20 instead of £24, you've still spent £20 you didn't plan on spending. If you are after something in particular, such as an electrical gadget, check prices before you go to make sure the airport price is the best deal.

6. Pretty kitty

Holidaying with your mates is brilliant. Who doesn't want to spend a concentrated amount of time with their friends in the sunshine, drinking sangria? The only problem is that it can cost a fortune.

Putting money into a kitty is one way to make your money go further. Pooling resources means you're all spending the same amount, so you won't be left holding a £40 round of Sambucas at the end of the night.

7. Stay sun safe

Being pale, I'm always careful in the sun and reapply sunscreen religiously. All the sunscreen I've ever bought is factor 50 and I've been known to buy children's factor 50-plus too. But it's not just the factor that you should take into account.

The factor covers UVB rays (the ones that burn you), but when it comes to UVA rays (the ones that cause wrinkles) you need to check the star rating on the back of the bottle. You'd think that fancy, more expensive brands would have the highest five-star rating but I've found Boots Essential range is the best value, at £1.50 per 100ml for the kids' factor 50 sunscreen, and has a high star rating.

8. Breakfast in bed

Breakfast may be the most important meal of the day but it can also be the most expensive if you are on holiday. I like to use Airbnb when I go on holiday because it's cheap and many places also give you access to cooking facilities. I like to make sure the places I book have self-catering facilities and I usually use the kitchen to prepare breakfast.

There always seems to be a huge mark-up on breakfast foods when you eat in a café; I just don't think it's good value to pay café prices for a couple of croissants and coffee when you can buy exactly the same at a local supermarket for a fraction of the price.

Trying local food is one of the best bits of going abroad, I know, but save your money for lunch and dinner.

THE
NO
SPEND
YEAR

FANCY
SOME
FREE
MONEY

FANCY SOME FREE MONEY?

Who doesn't like free stuff (you all know I do)? Getting free money may seem like wishful thinking, but you'd be surprised how much free money people give away each year. And you may be one of them.

In order to get this free money you have to save into a pension.

Let's face it, pensions aren't sexy; in fact they're downright boring. Few people bother to set one up themselves.

The government acknowledges that, so in 2012 it introduced 'auto-enrolment', which forces all employers to automatically enrol workers into a pension, and hopefully prevent us all from living in poverty in old age.

This means your employer will put you into a pension if you're aged over twenty-two and earning over £10,000 a year, but you'll have to pay a certain percentage of your income into the pension. At the moment the contribution you have to pay is very low – just 0.8% of your salary between £5,824 and £43,000 – but it will increase to 4% of salary by 2019.

The best thing is that, if you pay in to your pension, then so must your employer, and the government also gives you a contribution in the form of tax relief. This is based on your income tax – if your top rate of tax is 20%, you get 20% tax relief, and if you're a 40% higher rate income taxpayer you get 40%; if you pay 45% tax then you receive 45% relief.

What is tax relief?

Tax relief is a confusing term because if you think of tax, you tend to think of the government taking money off you.
In fact, tax relief is a reward for doing the right thing and

---

saving for old age. You pay your pension contribution out of your wages before the income tax is taken. So when the taxman takes his share you are effectively avoiding paying income tax on the sum that was placed into your pension.

This means your pension contribution is relieved of income tax. The amount of relief you are entitled to depends on the highest rate of income tax you pay: 20%, 40% or 45%.

This is essentially free money from your employer and the government – but if you don't pay into the pension, your employer and the government don't have to either.

Under the auto-enrolment rules, employees are allowed to opt out of the pension but, considering that if you do you'll be losing contributions from both your employer and the government, it's wise not to.

Next step

Now I've got you to think about saving, I'm going to tell you an important next step: save more.

By 2019, you'll be making a contribution of 4% of your salary into your workplace pension, your employer will have to contribute 3% and the government will reward you with 1% tax relief. Of course, you can contribute more if you want; that's up to you. If you do want to pay more you should speak to your HR department at work.

This means that a total contribution of 8% of your salary will be going into your pension. It's good but I'm sorry to tell you it's not enough.

The government is trying to ease us into saving but the truth is 8% isn't going to cut it. Most pension experts say that in order to have a decent retirement, you need a 15% pension contribution.

It's unlikely that your employer will increase their contribution beyond what the government tells them to pay, so instead you'll have to boost the amount of money that you put into your pension yourself.

The truth is that we have to take responsibility for our pensions and if we don't save enough when we're working neither employers nor the state will help us out when we're old.

Disclaimer: I only have £7,000 in my pension and stopped saving into one when I started working for myself as being self-employed I obviously don't receive employer contributions.

WHAT IS THE STOCK MARKET?

You've probably seen *The Wolf of Wall Street* and think the stock market is just lots of men in brightly coloured blazers shouting 'Sell, sell' and 'Buy, buy' down the telephone.

Forget that. The stock market is for everyone, regardless of whether they have a yellow blazer or not.

The stock market is an exchange where 'stocks', more commonly known as 'shares', in publicly held companies are bought and sold. It's worth noting that stocks and shares can also be called 'equities'.

The aim of the stock market is to make money. You hope that the shares you buy will go up in value and become worth more than you bought them for – and that the value won't fall. Lots of things can make shares go up and down, including changes in the economy, within the company, politics, regulation and consumer sentiment.

Investing in shares can make you money in two ways:

1. The company does well and the value of the stock rises (known as a capital gain)
2. The company pays a dividend to investors when it's doing well (this is paid as income but can be 'reinvested'; used to buy more shares)

However, investing in shares involves taking risk: the rewards are good but you could also stand to lose money if the value falls, and there is no guarantee of a dividend.

In the UK, the major exchange is the London Stock Exchange, which produces a number of indices that track different types of companies. The most well-known index is the FTSE 100, which is made up of the 100 largest companies in the UK based on market capitalisation (that's the number of shares the company has issued multiplied by the share price).

The companies in an index change all the time depending on how well those companies are doing. For instance, the FTSE 100 is rejigged every quarter to ensure that the companies included are still the 100 biggest, as one company may have lost or gained significant value, which would change its place in the index. Similarly, if there is a big takeover or merger within the index then this could affect a company's placing.

Investing money in shares is a gamble but the more risk you take, the more reward is on offer.

The stock market isn't always a smooth ride up and you could see the value of your investment fall. The good news is, history tells us that over the long term, investing in shares is a good bet – you just have to be willing to tie your money up for at least five to ten years (possibly longer) and ride out the tough times (and keep investing when shares are down, i.e. cheap) in order to benefit.

The 'Brexit' vote was a good example of just how volatile the stock market can be. The FTSE 100 fell 8% after the shock news that the UK had voted to leave the European Union – this means the value of the UK's largest companies fell by 8%.

And it wasn't just the UK that felt the pain of the vote; a total of $2 trillion was wiped off stock markets around the world, showing just how global and interconnected business is.

However, less than a week later the stock market had recovered and was trading at a higher level than before the vote. If you had panicked when the stock market fell 8% and taken all of your money out, you would have not only lost money because the value of your stocks had fallen (known as crystallising your losses), but you would also have missed out on the rally in the stocks when they went back up. Sharp peaks and troughs are exactly why you should plan to invest in the stock market for the long term, and keep investing when the going gets tough.

—— —— ——

THE
NO
SPEND
YEAR

—— —

THE BARE
MINIMUM:
BUDGET
BEAUTY

—— —— ——

'Are you sure you want me to do this?' he asked for what felt like the hundredth time.

'Yes. Just do it. It's only hair – it'll grow back,' I replied, more confidently than I felt.

The whirr of the clippers began and I felt the juddering of the metal on my skull. I heard Frank take a deep breath and he started to run the clippers over the back of my head, the hair falling to the bathroom floor.

I don't think any man really wants to cut his wife's hair – there's too much at stake – but without the option of visiting a hairdresser, I was willing to put my marriage on the line in an effort to tame my unruly mop.

Pamper days, beauty treatments and spending hours at the hairdresser have never been my idea of fun. I'm rubbish with eyeliner and my chipped toenail polish leaves a lot to be desired.

Giving up the lax health and beauty regime I had in place for a year wouldn't be a hardship, I thought; I probably wouldn't even notice. I was pretty sure that I didn't really spend any money on beauty whatnots and health.

Except when I added it up, I'd spent nearly £450 the year before my challenge on exercise classes, special shampoos, new perfume, make-up, miracle creams and bikini waxes. Not to mention the constant battle with the hair on my head.

OK, maybe I was wrong about the beauty stuff but I knew that I didn't spend a lot on clothes. My wardrobe was less than half the size of my sister's and I owned far less clothing than my friends. I'd made a concerted effort to reduce the items in my wardrobe in my quest for minimalism and I'd done a good job (I thought), other than the cycle-related clothing that seemed to dominate several bedroom drawers.

Wrong again. Some more sums showed I'd spent £550 on clothes in the previous year. Beauty, health and clothes had cost me £1,000, and I hadn't even realised I was spending the money. A few quid on an impulsively bought mascara, a tube of a cream that I'd used once, and exercise classes at the gym which I had only attended a handful of times had all pushed the bill up.

Maybe I had placed more emphasis on looking and smelling nice than I'd thought. I'd definitely spent a lot of money on my health, beauty products and clothes. And in that case, how would I feel when I neither looked nor smelt very nice?

I can give you that answer now: I felt terrible.

My appearance went downhill pretty soon after I started the challenge. Being out on my bike every day in the cold and wind and lashing rain took its toll quickly. By Christmas I was a wind-whipped mess with ruddy, dry skin and a deep-red nose that wouldn't have looked out of place on Rudolph.

Just to kick a woman when she's down, it was around December that any nice lotions and potions I did already own started to run out. I cut open the tubes of moisturiser and eye creams, scraping every last drop out in a bid to revitalise my sad complexion.

As part of my grocery budget I could buy basic toiletries, but I'd put little thought into what toiletries would count as basics and what the essentials exactly were. Of course, everything I was going to buy would be from Lidl, the cheapest supermarket near me, but even they have their own range of fancy creams and hair treatments. Just because it was in Lidl and didn't cost a lot didn't make something an essential (if that was the case I would have spent my whole food budget buying wine).

After a lot of scouring of the toiletries aisle in Lidl I decided that there were few toiletries I actually needed. Yes, I would have liked to buy an exfoliating face scrub or a hair masque but I could live without them.

This is the list of toiletries I decided was essential:

Shampoo 65p
Conditioner 65p
Toothpaste 55p
Toothbrush 79p for two
Soap 79p for four bars
Deodorant 59p
Razors 79p for 10

Even if I had to buy all these toiletries at the same time, the total cost would be just £4.81.

The only other personal care items that I purchased were cotton buds, loo rolls and tampons.

Some people questioned whether conditioner or razors were essential but I was happy with the amount by which I'd stripped back my spending on smellies.

Over the year I purchased:

5 x bottles of shampoo = £3.25
5 x bottles of conditioner = £3.25
6 x tubes of toothpaste = £3.30
3 x packs of toothbrushes = £2.37
6 x packs of soap = £3.95
6 x deodorants = £2.95
4 x packs of razors = £3.16

The total cost of all my toiletries for the year was £22.23, which is 5% of my total spend on toiletries in the year before.

OK, I could have swapped the shampoo and soap for a bottle of washing-up liquid and spent even less, but I'll settle for a saving of 95% on my previous spending!

The one thing I did wrestle with when it came to essentials was moisturiser; believe me, I never thought a cheap moisturiser would cause me so much angst. I toed and froed over whether it was an essential and finally decided it wasn't.

I quickly regretted the decision to exclude it as an essential. I have dry skin as it is, but add poor weather and cycling into the mix and my face was as dry as the Sahara – I swear the number of wrinkles I had doubled in the six weeks between the beginning of the challenge and Christmas.

My face, lips and hands were cracked and dry. I looked a right mess by the end of the year. Although no one said anything, I'm sure they noticed but were just too polite to ask what the bloody hell had happened to my face.

With a few days indoors over the Christmas holidays, I decided to try out some home-made beauty treatments using what I had in the cupboards and fridge. I figured if I had a terrible reaction or tinted my face a weird colour in the name of experimentation, then at least I wouldn't have to see anyone or leave the house for a bit.

After some furious Googling of home-made moisturisers, I realised that all the 'simple and natural' recipes relied on the purchase of some expensive ingredients like tubs of coconut oil or shea butter, with different combinations of natural oils such as lavender or vanilla added to them. I hadn't been able to bring myself to spend £1 on a tub of moisturiser; why would I buy all that stuff!

Annoyed with my failed Internet search, I went into the kitchen instead in search of stuff to slap on my face. After a few minutes standing in front of the fridge with a tub of butter in my hand trying to decide if it was a good idea to put it on my face, a bunch of bananas caught my eye.

Bananas are a bit slimy; that could be moisturising? They're also natural so nothing could go wrong, right? Don't you get potassium poisoning if you eat too many bananas? Can you get potassium poisoning by rubbing bananas on your face?

'Sod it', I thought and started to peel a ripe banana. I chopped it up, put it in a bowl and mushed it up with a fork. It didn't really look like a face mask but I took it to the bathroom anyway and started slathering the cold goo on my face.

I can't tell you if rubbing banana over your face is a wonder moisturiser because after a couple of minutes the smell of banana was so overpowering I thought I was going to puke and had to furiously wash the stuff off; clumps of banana clogged up the plughole which made me heave again.

Conclusion: bananas are for eating.

It was a failed first attempt but I wasn't deterred. I went back to the fridge to look at the butter again. No, I definitely wasn't going to use that. Then I had a brainwave: olive oil.

Surely that's just as good as using coconut oil or almond oil or any of the other expensive oils out there? To be honest I don't know why I didn't think of it first.

Armed with some olive oil (£2.79 for a big bottle at Lidl, if you're interested) and some kitchen roll, I decanted a bit of the oil and started to dab my face. After I'd done that I just sat there. I didn't really have a plan; should I leave it to soak in or wash it off? How long should I leave it on for?

I guessed about five minutes and then I used some warm water to wash the excess off my face and dabbed my face dry, ruining a towel in the process (maybe I should have washed my face more thoroughly).

Ignoring the stained towel, I peered at my skin closely in the mirror, my nose almost touching it. Did I look moisturised? I felt a bit greasy but actually, yes it was sort of moisturised.

Of course I don't slather myself in olive oil every morning and then trot off to work, but I do oil my face a couple of nights a week to try to keep the dry skin at bay. I wouldn't recommend using the oil on your face when it's hot outside though; I was worried I'd fry my skin and go from cracked and dry to crisp and dry.

Encouraged by the success of the olive oil moisturiser, I decided to add some to a couple of tablespoons of brown sugar and use it as an exfoliator. It worked really well (although it was a bit too harsh for my face), leaving my skin nice and smooth; but the downside was the scummy ring it left round the bath. And the oil clogged the plug a bit. Grim.

The sugar scrub may have been a bit harsh for my skin but later I found an exfoliator that wasn't: the humble oat. A cheap packet of oats plus water equals a brilliant face scrub. The oats are tough enough to get rid of dry skin and when you rub the paste into your face it has an almost milky feel that is extremely moisturising. My friend Cat wasn't so convinced of its merits when we mucked around with it on a girly sleepover, mostly because it smelt and felt horrible, but the outcome was good. Definitely try it!

Eight months into my challenge I was given some respite from my home-made potions thanks to a chance conversation with a colleague about Botox. She's a self-confessed beauty junkie (and Botox aficionado) and couldn't believe I'd been washing my face with soap and putting olive oil on my skin.

Very kindly she offered to give me a couple of face masks that she had going spare, telling me she'd send them to me.

A couple of days later a shoebox turned up at my house packed with a selection of beauty products. It turned out another of her colleagues was moving house and was clearing out her rather large stash of goodies. There were trial pots of serums and moisturisers (hoorah!) as well as toners and some hair products. Oh, and of course, the face masks.

I don't think I've ever put so many products on my face in one evening. Although I'd never been bothered about beauty – or so I'd thought – I was like a kid in a sweet shop. I was so exuberant that the products ran out after a few months, but they got me to October, which I was extremely grateful for – and for which my skin was even more grateful.

Talking to my friends about the generosity of the two ladies who sent me the toiletries, I was amazed when they started to admit that they too hoarded beauty products and had bottles knocking about in the back of their bathroom cupboards that they'd only used once.

Toiletries are pretty cheap in relation to new shoes or a jacket, and you can pick them up with your coffee and baked beans when you do a supermarket shop, so it's no surprise really that people build up a cosmetics collection to rival Superdrug. If the product you bought isn't for you or doesn't do what it says it will (which happens often in my experience!) then you've only spent a few quid so it doesn't feel like a huge loss.

Except it does add up and we end up losing money and gaining tubes of lotions we've only used half of. Those pesky advertisers know exactly how to squeeze money out of us and even though I know there isn't a lipstick in the world that can make me look like Scarlett Johansson, for the sake of a fiver buying the lipstick might bring me a step closer.

It's safe to say that, after a year without a proper moisturiser and with a make-up bag that looks very sorry for itself, I'm even further away from looking like Scarlett Johansson.

I've never worn make-up every day because, in all honesty, I'm too lazy. I'd love to be one of those groomed women who make the effort with their hair and nails and always sport beautifully made-up faces, but it's just not in my DNA to get up early and slap a face on.

That doesn't mean I don't like to make the effort now and again, rocking out the foundation, concealer, highlighter, mascara and lippie for the right occasion. The only problem with doing that when the occasion did present itself, in the form of weddings, christenings, birthday parties and black tie work dinners, was that my foundation and concealer had bitten the dust by the end of January.

I hadn't quite appreciated that make-up goes off. My foundation and concealer I had had for a while, admittedly, but you'd have thought I'd bought them a decade ago looking at the weird watery gloop they both turned into. Trying to get them to stay on my face and not run down to my chin was a challenge in itself, and even when I did get them to stick they made my face look as if it was peeling away.

You'll agree that 'zombie' isn't a great look for a christening, so they both went in the bin and I had to rely on my mascara and lipstick for the rest of the year. I could take some comfort (I think) in Frank's rather backhanded compliment: 'Don't worry, you look better without make-up now than you did before'.

I can't work out if I still looked bad but not as bad as before, or whether I looked OK bare-faced but I should put some make-up on anyway . . . Still, probably best not to dig around that 'compliment' too much!

HAIR SCARE

When it comes to patience my husband should probably win an award, considering how understanding and helpful he's been through my no spend challenge. But he should probably also receive a bravery award for cutting my hair.

I've kept my hair short for a number of years now, which is a lot of work in terms of haircuts. Thankfully my sister Kerry trained as a hairdresser so whenever I'd go to see her I'd get her to trim my hair, and a couple of times a year I'd book into a salon to have it cut there. If I knew I wasn't going to see my sister for a bit then having the option of the hairdressing salon was handy, even though it cost about £40 a time.

Haircuts are expensive enough, let alone having your hair dyed at a salon, so I've always dyed my own at home each month with the £5 kits you get from the supermarket. I enjoy chopping and changing colours – and as I've got older the dye has become essential for covering up the increasing number of grey hairs.

My twice-yearly salon visits and home hair-dyeing weren't essentials though, so for the year of the challenge, they were out.

On reflection I should have dyed my hair before I stopped spending, but it didn't cross my mind until about two weeks into the challenge when I noticed my terrible roots. I wish I was better at planning ahead.

Short hair always seems to grow much more quickly than long hair, and it wasn't long before I really needed a trim. Luckily Kerry came to my house over the Christmas period and was able to make me look a bit respectable, but our visits to one another this year wouldn't be as frequent as usual because I'd have to cycle to her house and she lives around thirty miles away.

That's when Frank had to get brave and start helping me keep my hair in check by trimming the back and sides with the clippers he uses to do his own hair. I find that if the back and sides of my hair are neat I can get away with growing the top out a bit.

And do you know what, he does a bloody good job at barbering my hair. In fact, so good that he might have to keep doing it for ever (or at least until he takes a chunk out of my hair or ear!).

So, haircuts were covered, but what about hair dye? I wondered if I could just stop dyeing it and embrace my natural mousey colour, tinged with grey; I looked a mess anyway, so what did it matter that my hair looked drab too?

But the challenge was to keep living my life happily and I don't think walking around with terrible hair would have made me happy. Lots of people had recommended getting my hair cut and coloured by a student hairdresser. Apparently colleges are always looking for people to practise on and the cuts and colours are supervised by tutors, so not that much can go wrong.

The only downside, I was told, is that the appointments took a lot longer than normal and what would have been an hour and a half appointment at an ordinary salon would take about three hours. It still seemed like a good deal to me, though, so I started the hunt for colleges and hairdressing academies.

There's no shortage of people who want to cut your hair for free (which would have been great if I didn't have a husband with clippers), but the colours would cost – only £10 in some cases, but a cost nonetheless.

I didn't make it to a hairdressing college for a free haircut either; I found that the times they needed models just didn't fit with my schedule. But if you're more flexible than me and willing to let a trainee practise on you, then you'll be rewarded with a free haircut and a reduced-price colour.

I'd almost resigned myself to sporting my natural hair colour for a year (something I haven't done since I was seventeen) and was lamenting the fact on Twitter when a kind woman (another Michelle) offered me her stash of hair dye – for nothing.

Michelle told me that she had decided to embrace her grey hair and, as far as she was concerned, sending me her leftover hair dye was recycling as it would go in the bin otherwise. I jumped at the chance and she sent me three home dye kits in a lovely shade of brown.

When the parcel arrived from this hair dye angel I realised I hadn't even asked what colour it was! But I think I would have dyed my hair any colour at that stage just to get rid of my mousey locks.

The three kits lasted me until the end of the year, as I stretched them out by only dyeing my hair once every two months. Thank you, Michelle! Your kindness meant my clippered hair actually looked like a style.

And while we're talking about hair, the razors tackled my legs and armpits but if you're a lady reading this you'll know razors aren't ideal for other areas! There wasn't much I could do about my bikini line; I didn't fancy melting down tea lights to try to fashion some sort of wax strip.

I did hear that the British cycling team who went to the Rio Olympics were put on a bikini wax ban, as more hair equals fewer saddle sores and more gold medals, so in a way I was ahead of the curve (and I haven't had any saddle sores all year!).

FASHION VICTIM

I may have been trendsetting when it came to my bikini line but I can assure you that when it came to fashion my outfits won't be appearing in *Vogue* any time soon – unless they do a scruffy cyclist special.

It was obvious that my clothes and shoes would wear a bit thin as the year went on, but cycling accelerated the demise of my wardrobe. Most of the time I'm on my bike I'm wearing cycling shorts, a cycle T-shirt and, if it's cold, my cycle-specific zip-up top and jacket, as well as leggings when it's really chilly.

My cycling gear was the first casualty of the no spend year as my leggings, as I've already mentioned, have what can only be described as an obscene rip up the leg and crotch, as well as two worn patches on each bum cheek. Thankfully I had cycling shorts to wear underneath.

As the year wore on the zip on my zip-up top decided it didn't want to zip any more, I lost one of my gloves, I lost my neck warmer and I lost my arm warmers. All extremely annoying incidents but probably not as annoying as when my non-bike clothes took a turn for the worse.

If you look scruffy riding a bike, so what? You're exercising, so of course you're not going to look perfect.

Of course cycling is going to wear down my cycling clothes;

but it also knackered my normal clothes. Sometimes there wasn't anywhere suitable to change in and out of my cycle gear when I went to meetings or out with my friends, so I'd wear my everyday clothes – typically jeans and a T-shirt – on my bike. There were also lots of times I just couldn't be bothered to take a spare change of clothes with me, so I can't blame my bike totally.

I didn't think riding in my everyday clothes would be a huge problem, but it quickly became one. All my jeans looked terrible from quite early on; every pair now sports a saddle mark on the backside, and one pair have worn through and have a nice laddered effect in the bum.

And my T-shirts didn't fare any better either. In short: they stink of BO. I know that isn't a pleasant thing to admit but they all now have that ingrained BO smell under the arms that no amount of washing will get out. It's gross, it's my own fault and I felt so embarrassed at times because I knew I was turning up to events stinking and 100 layers of deodorant were doing nothing to mask the pong.

The less said about my holey pants and socks the better. Thankfully very few people see them!

I smelt bad and looked terrible. At first I just shrugged it off with a joke about my 'new look' for the next year, but it did start to get me down.

There was just no point trying to look nice for something when I knew I had to get on a bike, get sweaty, have my make-up run down my face and my clothes start to stink. I did start to feel embarrassed.

I wouldn't say I was precious about my appearance before the challenge but I started to feel more and more that I wanted to stay inside and hide. I had to wear practical clothing that would get me from A to B and that started to wear on my confidence after a while. Some days I just wanted to dress up, get on the bus and go to an event, without helmet hair and sweat patches.

Dressing like a scruff-bag for a year has had a plus side though. I've learned two important things; the first is that quality trumps quantity.

I used to buy cheap clothing and it hasn't lasted. My £5 T-shirts have stretched out of shape and the material has become thinner and thinner. The cheap trainers I had fell apart pretty quickly, with the rubber sole peeling away from the canvas shoes and a large hole appearing in the bottom of the trainer.

Granted, I'd bought all of these clothes well before the challenge – I didn't buy a whole new wardrobe just before I stopped spending – but they didn't last as long as I thought they would.

In contrast, the DhB brand cycling shorts I have, which at £70 were an expensive buy, have lasted really well. I baulked at paying that much for cycling shorts when I got them, but they're still going strong and are nowhere near needing replacing despite the thousands of miles I've cycled.

The second thing I've learned is that I don't actually need that many clothes. I already had a pretty compact wardrobe when the challenge started but I've managed to pare it back further, donating clothes to charity that I no longer wear.

I wear a pretty standard uniform of jeans and T-shirts with trainers or boots and really they're the only things I need to replace. Oh, and a new going-out dress; my one dress has inexplicably got what looks like bike oil over it. I have no idea how that happened . . .

I don't actually need that many items, but when I do replace those things I'll do it with more expensive, better-quality items that will last.

NO GYM REQUIRED

Over the past year I may have looked an absolute state but there was a definite positive to cycling everywhere: I've never been as fit.

Although I haven't kept an exact record, my conservative estimate is that I've cycled 6,500 miles this year. For hardcore cyclists this won't sound very much and for others it will seem like a ludicrous amount. For me, it's quite a lot and certainly more than I've done in any other year.

It's no surprise then that I lost about a stone in weight, going from just over 11 stone to just over 10 stone.

The step up in exercise wasn't the only reason I lost weight, though. By having to meal plan and stick to essentials we no longer bought pre-packaged food or treats, which meant that I was eating more basic but still nutritious meals containing lots of vegetables, lentils and rice – all cheap ingredients that can be cooked in various ways.

I also drank a lot less alcohol and caffeine and lots more water and it must have done some good, as I've been told by lots of people that not spending money suits me and I look healthier than I have done in a while.

Cycling everywhere was obviously my main form of exercise, but it's nice to mix up the exercise now and again. I couldn't pay for classes or gym sessions any longer, so I had to find free exercise classes that would give my body a break from cycling.

Exercise classes can be expensive and I thought that it would be impossible to find cheap, let alone free, ones. Again that was my laziness showing through; I'd never bothered to look for free classes so I didn't know they existed, but they do.

My best London find is Our Parks, which runs free fitness sessions in parks around the capital – you can do everything from boxercise to yoga, with the added bonus of getting to meet people from your local community.

Although Our Parks is run only in London in conjunction with local councils, there are council-run programmes around the country offering free and cheap classes. For example, Manchester City Council has an 'active lifestyles' programme with over 150 fitness and well-being sessions available each week for just £1.

It's also worth checking out local branches of Lululemon and Sweaty Betty, both of which sell workout gear. The clothing is eye-wateringly expensive but they offer free classes. While Lululemon focuses on yoga, Sweaty Betty has barre classes, Pilates and boot camps to name just a few – although what is on offer depends on the area you live in.

I was quite intimidated about going to these classes in my worn-out leggings but although there are some people there who have bought the whole range of branded leggings and tops, no one cares what you're wearing; they're all too focused on their downward dogs.

If you too feel intimidated by the idea of joining classes full of yoga-honed bodies, and want to work out on your own without the cost of expensive gym membership, then free gyms set up in local parks are actually pretty good. The machinery looks a bit clunky but it does the job and you don't have to tie yourself into a gym contract that costs you a fortune. I'd recommend checking out the NHS Choices website to find out what free facilities are available near you.

And if you're even more nervous about exercising and don't fancy doing it in front of other people at all, you can always use online tutorials and YouTube videos to get fit and build confidence, and maybe try going to a class later on. I couldn't believe the number of people offering online lessons for free, and was opened up to the world of yoga tutorials by my friend Emmylou who is training to become a yoga teacher (so I must admit I have been lucky and I've also benefited from some free private lessons!).

My yoga moves still leave a lot to be desired but my back has been thankful for the stretching, especially after long miles in the bike saddle.

Staying healthy doesn't have to cost the earth. I feel great, and it's thanks to the wealth of resources available for free – the only thing you have to bring along is the motivation to exercise. Feeling healthy does make me happy and I'm grateful that my body has propelled me thousands of miles on a bike this year and has got stronger, rather than deteriorated.

Good health is all anyone can wish for but I won't pretend that I was unaffected by the way I looked over the last year. I don't think I'm a vain person but it was difficult to embrace looking like I'd been pulled through a hedge backwards for twelve months.

There were plenty of times I wished the ground would open up and swallow me whole, usually when I turned up to black tie events, donned my crumpled dress out of my rucksack, and tried to smooth my hair into place. Hopefully people noticed how scruffy I looked but not how bad I smelt!

BUDGET BEAUTY AND HALF-PRICE HEALTH

Looking and feeling good doesn't have to cost a fortune provided you have the motivation to make some changes.

1. Sugar baby

Sugar and olive oil are my go-to ingredients when it comes to home-made beauty treatments. Forget forking out on expensive body scrubs; you can't go wrong with sugar and oil mixed together. It will give you amazingly smooth skin. Be careful about using this on your face though, if your skin is sensitive.

2. Swap shop

Whether it's clothes or beauty products, I bet you have a load of stuff in your cupboards that you no longer use or you don't like. Why not have a swap night with your mates where you can pick and choose from each other's clothing and beauty cast-offs? An eyeshadow that looks terrible on you may look fab on a friend.

3. Quality not quantity

It's easy to get lured in by the cheap clothes on offer in the shops these days but is it really good value if a £5 T-shirt falls apart after three washes? Falling into the trap of buying lots of cheap clothing isn't good for the environment or your pocket; more expensive, quality clothing will last longer and save you money in the long run.

4. Make-up magic

Two tricks I learned this year to get the most out of your make-up: when your mascara dries up, put it into a glass of warm water. This magically unclogs the mascara at the bottom of the tube. And if your lipstick breaks (in my case my only lipstick), warm the broken ends over a flame and stick them back together.

5. Neat feet

Pedicures can be expensive but if you want smooth tootsies, just rub some cheap-as-chips Vaseline over your feet, pop some socks on and leave for a few hours. Don't try to walk around without the socks, you'll end up in A&E.

6. Scent sense

Another top tip for using Vaseline. If you rub a small amount behind your elbows, ears and wrists before you add your perfume, it makes your fragrance last much longer.

7. Got trainers? Use them

It doesn't take money to exercise, it takes motivation. If you have a body that works and a pair of trainers, then a brisk walk is fantastic exercise. Initiatives like Couch to 5K, which can be found on the NHS website, are great for those new to running who want to follow a structured programme.

8. Free apps

As well as online tutorials there are free apps that can help whip you into shape. I like cycling app Strava, which helps log your distance, and Freeletics, which provides you with free body-weight workouts that are as short as twenty minutes; they require no equipment and can be done in a small space.

9. Home-made equipment

If you're working out at home, running or cycling and feel like you want to push yourself a bit further, fill a couple of water bottles to make fantastic makeshift weights. OK, you won't build up Arnie-level muscles but it will intensify your workout.

10. Simple is best

The best type of beauty regime doesn't come from an expensive tube, it's something my mum has relied on for years: drink lots of water and get some sleep. Being knackered and dehydrated is never a good look.

THE
NO
SPEND
YEAR

INVESTING

INVESTING

Investing is usually seen as the preserve of the wealthy, something ordinary people can't afford to do. But that's a myth: if you save into a pension it's likely that you're already investing and just don't know about it, so there's no harm in learning the basics.

Asset classes

The cornerstones of investing are 'asset classes', of which there are four main types. Assets are what you invest your money in with the hope that those assets will provide a return for you – in other words, make you money.

1. The first asset class (and one that I've touched on already) is equities, also known as stocks or shares.

    Shares in publicly held companies can be bought and sold and the idea is to buy them at a cheaper price, see their value rise and then sell them when the price is higher. While you hold on to the shares you may also receive a 'dividend' – basically an income payment from the company to keep you sweet.

2. Fixed income investments make up the second asset class on our list. These investments, commonly known as 'bonds', are very different to shares.

    Instead of buying a stake in a company, bonds allow you to loan money to a company.

    You hand your money over and the company gives you an IOU that promises to pay your money back at a set time in the future. Up until that point it will pay you interest (known as a 'coupon') at certain points (maybe every six months or every year) until it has to pay back the original amount loaned at the pre-set date.

The higher the interest offered the more risky the bond, which means the greater the chance the company won't be able to either pay the interest or pay back the original loan at the date set out.

You can buy bonds from the government – called 'gilts' – which are pretty much risk-free (the government isn't likely to default on a payment), but these offer an extremely low coupon or interest.

Bonds are seen as less risky than equities because you know what interest payment you will get (whereas you don't know what dividend you will get, if any) and you can expect to get your money back at a certain point, whereas if a share price falls you could lose a large chunk of money in equities.

3. You probably already own some of this asset class: cash. The returns you get on cash aren't great and even though you may think putting your money in the bank is risk-free, it's not.

    The biggest risk to cash savings is inflation: the cost of goods, services and general living. Over time the cost of living creeps up, meaning the value of your cash is worth less over time – £1,000 would have bought far more in 2000 than it would today and if that £1,000 had been left in the bank since 2000 its value would have eroded.

4. Alternative investments make up the fourth corner of asset classes. Things that don't neatly fit into shares, bonds or cash can be classed under this heading, including property, commodities (like oil) and hedge funds. These asset classes are typically more illiquid than the other three assets, meaning they are harder to sell, making them more risky.

Diversification

Diversification is a fancy way to say 'Don't put all your eggs in one basket' when it comes to where you invest. It's good to have a mix of equities, bonds, cash and even some alternative investments as they all do different things and have different levels of risk.

It's not only asset classes that should be diversified. It's where you invest within the asset classes too.

For example, if you're investing in equities you don't want to put all your money into UK pharmaceutical company shares because if something happens to UK pharmaceuticals you could lose a lot or all of your money.

You could diversify by instead investing in lots of different types of UK companies and also by moving outside of the UK to invest in other parts of the world.

So how do I buy all these things?

It's unlikely that you'll have the expertise to buy lots of individual shares and bonds – I certainly don't.

Thankfully, there are clever people called fund managers who can do this for you. This is called active fund management, as the fund manager actively picks and chooses investments to buy and sell.

You give them your money by investing in their fund and they pool all of the investors' money together and use it to buy stocks, bonds, cash, alternative investments or a mix of some or all of them, to try to make your money grow.

What they invest in depends on their specialism and the fund's remit. Some fund managers specialise by geographic region: UK, North America, India, emerging markets etc.

Others specialise by company sector: biotechnology, small and mid-sized companies, or mining.

And other funds have totally different targets based on

achieving a set level of income, or they invest money to ensure they do not overshoot a certain level of risk.

There are thousands of funds on offer, all with a different 'investment mandate' and charging different fees; but all the managers have one aim – to make money.

Active versus passive

Giving your savings to an active fund manager isn't the only way to invest. Many argue that active fund management can be expensive because not only do you have to pay the manager but it also costs the fund whenever a manager makes a trade, all of which eat into your profit.

This is why passive investment is growing in popularity. Passive funds, which are also known as trackers, in their most simple form track an index.

For example, take a passive fund that tracks the FTSE 100: it would invest in all 100 companies in that index with the amount invested in each company representative of where they are in the index (so, investing more in the company at the top of the FTSE 100 than the company at the bottom).

The investment changes depending on movement of companies up and down the index and if a company dropped out of the FTSE 100 then the passive fund wouldn't hold it any more.

There are thousands of indices around the world being tracked by thousands of different passive funds and it is a growing market. Lots of people are keen on passives because they are far cheaper than actively managed funds, as there's no manager to pay.

There is also an argument that the majority of fund managers are failing to beat the stock market anyway, so investors may as well invest in a tracker and just take the return offered, rather than paying someone money to try to outperform the market.

Risk

Investing is inherently risky but you can choose how much risk to take, with shares and alternative investments being more risky, as we've seen, than bonds and cash.

However, the more risk you are willing to take the more reward you could receive. Don't ever believe anyone who tells you they can get you a hefty 8% return a year risk-free; they're either lying or an idiot.

Taking risk isn't black and white: it's not a choice between taking loads of risk and none at all; there are varying degrees of risk tolerance.

There are loads of online tools available from different fund groups and financial advisers that will allow you to test your risk tolerance. Some will even provide a steer towards the types of investments that could suit you.

If you're really unsure about where you should invest to match your tolerance level then a robo-advice service could be a good start. These online advice services are cheaper than face-to-face advice and for a small fee will take you through your investment objectives, risk tolerance and investment options.

Remember the rules

Investing can make for a bumpy ride and at times it can test your nerve. There are a few rules that you should stick by.

1. Set a goal: investing without an aim means you're more likely to dip into the money (the same goes for saving); it's best to put your money to work to try to achieve something, such as investing for retirement.
2. Realise you're not going to become a millionaire overnight: investing is for the long term and you'll have to stay invested for at least five years to see a real benefit.

3. Stay invested when things get rough: the worst thing you can do is take your money out of the stock market when it's down, as you could end up with less than your original investment.
4. Know when to invest more: it may feel counter-intuitive but when the stock markets are going through a rough patch you should invest more and when prices are high, start selling. Most people don't and end up buying high and selling low, which is the worst thing you can do.
5. Drip feed money in: it's best to invest into the stock market regularly (e.g., by putting £50 into a fund every month). No one can time the market to put a big lump sum into a fund at exactly the right time (i.e. when the stock market is cheap), so it's best to spread your bets and invest steadily over time.

HOW TO BE A TAX AVOIDER (TOTALLY LEGALLY)

The first thing to point out is that tax avoidance is legal, tax evasion is definitely not.

I want you to become a tax avoider. No, I don't mean employing armies of people to help you find loopholes in the UK tax rules and systematically exploit them in order to pay next to nothing into the collective pot (you know who you are, big conglomerates that rhyme with Schmoogle and Hard-Lucks).

I'm talking about making the most of the legal tax breaks that are in place to boost your savings.

If you're saving money then that's fantastic, but *where* you save can really make a difference to your overall stash.

* Don't feel intimidated by the different ways to save – imagine your money in a pot and the way you save is just a bunch of tax rules that sit around the money that provide different rewards and tax reliefs – once you understand the rules you'll know where best to put your money *

Bank accounts

Most people put their cash in the bank, which is fine if it's your emergency money that you need to access quickly (just make sure you shop around for the best level of interest rather than defaulting to your current bank account).

One other very recent benefit to saving in a bank account is that you can now earn £1,000 interest on your bank account each year without paying any tax if you're a basic rate taxpayer (paying 20% tax) or £500 a year if you're a higher rate taxpayer (paying 40%).

Previously, the interest earned on your bank balance was taxed at your highest level of income tax, but the 'personal savings allowance' has taken that sting out of saving.

You'd need to save tens of thousands of pounds in the bank before hitting the £1,000 interest threshold, so you probably don't need to worry about your rainy-day fund being taxed just yet, but if you are a super-saver and have used up your £1,000 allowance you will have to arrange to pay your tax with HMRC as the tax isn't taken automatically from your bank account.

And if you are saving a small fortune into a bank account, remember that only the first £75,000 is protected under the Financial Services Compensation Scheme (FSCS). This means if you save £100,000 into your bank account and the bank goes bust, you'll only get £75,000 back from the scheme.

You can spread your savings around as banks have their own compensation limit, so if you had £75,000 in Bank A and £75,000 saved in Bank B and they both go bust then you'll get your full £150,000 back.

Please check when using multiple banks that they are not linked; the compensation is per institution not bank account. For instance, RBS and NatWest are part of the same banking group, so if you have £75,000 saved with each and they both go out of business then only £75,000 of your money is covered by the FSCS.

Individual Savings Accounts (ISA)

The ISA is an extremely popular way to save and lots of iterations have emerged to encourage more people to save and invest.

Bog-standard ISA

The basic ISA allows you to save money free of any tax – either income tax or capital gains tax (CGT), the latter of which is paid on the growth in value of the investments you hold, like shares. You pay into the ISA out of your wages (which will already have been taxed); any return you make in the ISA is tax-free and then when you take your money out it is also tax-free.

In the industry this is known as taxed-exempt-exempt (TEE).

The current savings allowance for the ISA is £15,240 but that is increasing to £20,000 in April 2017.

You can put your money into cash or into the stock market via the basic ISA, splitting your allowance whichever way you like: putting more into cash, or more into the stock market; or splitting it evenly between the two.

The interest you make in a cash ISA is free from income tax and the growth on stock-market investments is free from CGT, making ISAs a really good deal.

Not only are basic ISAs tax-free but you can access your money whenever you like, making them the go-to savings product.

Any saving is good but if you are planning on saving long-term – by which I mean for over five years – then it's a good idea to use your ISA to invest in the stock market. Cash rates on ISAs are stupidly low at the moment, and likely to remain low thanks to low interest rates, so if you want to make any return the stock market is a better option.

There are plenty of online investment platforms that will allow you to set up an ISA and make a regular payment into a fund or into individual stocks, allowing you to drip-feed money into the stock market and build up your savings.

Parents can also set up a junior ISA for their children and save up to £4,080 a year (less than an adult ISA) on their behalf. The children get control of the money at age eighteen but cannot take the money out before then. Other than the lower allowance and the fact that it cannot be accessed, you can invest a junior ISA in the same way as an adult ISA, putting the money in cash or stocks and shares.

Flexible ISA

This is a reasonably new addition to the ISA stable. Previously, if you took money out of an ISA you weren't allowed to pay it back in until the start of the following tax year, when the ISA limit resets itself. (It does this on 6 April each year – a weird date, I know; I'm not sure why!)

The flexible ISA allows you to pay money in and take it out, then pay it back in again (up to the ISA limit of course) without losing any of the tax-free allowance.

This is particularly good if you need to use your ISA money to cover an emergency and then put the money back in when you can, or if you need access to your savings from time to time.

Help-to-Buy ISA

If you're currently saving a deposit to buy your first home then there's a good chance you'll already have one of these ISAs. It aims to help people on to the housing ladder and lets you save up to £200 a month, with the added bonus that the government will give you another 25% – or up to £50 a month – top-up. Also, in the first month you can put in as much as £1,200.

The maximum bonus the government will give you is £3,000 and to receive it you would need to save £12,000 over five years into the ISA. The minimum government bonus that will be paid out is £400 so you have to save at least £1600 in order to claim it.

However, you shouldn't rely on the government's £3,000 bonus to become part of your deposit as it's only paid to you once the purchase is completed. Don't let this put you off though – that £3,000 could come in handy for redecorating, mortgage repayments or for overpaying the mortgage.

Lifetime ISA

This is the newest ISA on the market, and will be available from April 2017. It is aimed at those under forty and will, the government hopes, encourage younger people to save.

You will be able to save a maximum of £4,000 a year and the

government will give you a 25% top-up, meaning you receive £1 from the government for every £4 saved.

This might seem very generous but there is a catch: lifetime ISAs aren't going to be as flexible as a normal ISA. You will only be able to access the money either after you reach the age of sixty or to buy your first home, provided the home you are buying is worth less than £450,000.

If you take out your savings before the age of sixty and do not use them to buy a home, then the government will take back the bonus, plus any growth made on it, and levy a penalty of 5% on top of that. Ouch.

The severity of the charges is because the government wants you to either buy a home with the money saved or use it to fund your retirement. It doesn't want to give bonuses to people who are just going to spend the cash on a holiday.

* If you are currently using a help-to-buy ISA, the government has said you will be able to transfer the funds into a lifetime ISA, meaning you will be able to use the government bonus towards a house deposit *

Pensions

Pensions are something that bring most people out in a cold sweat; the rules seem complicated, and people are confused about where the money is and how to get hold of it.

The general rules are actually pretty simple and generally work in an opposite way to the TEE system of ISAs.

Let's assume you're paying into a workplace pension, which is how most people save for retirement. Your pension contribution will come out of the pension before you pay tax on your income, meaning the contribution is tax-free.

Any growth on your money inside a pension is also tax-free but when you take the money out to fund your retirement (which you can do from age fifty-five – although this figure is bound to be far higher by the time millennials reach retirement), you have to pay income tax on it.

This tax treatment is called exempt-exempt-taxed (EET) – basically the opposite of an ISA.

So why would you lock your money into a pension until you're fifty-five, or likely much older, if you could just save into an ISA instead? Well, the government gives you the incentive of tax relief.

It's a confusing term but it means that the government tops up your money as a reward for saving for your future. The bonus is set at the highest rate of income tax that you pay: one of 20%, 40% or 45%.

If you're saving through the workplace then your employer has to contribute too, meaning you get a double bonus. If you're not saving into a workplace pension then you're turning your nose up at free money from your boss and the government.

* You can currently save up to £40,000 a year into a pension (I wish) and £1 million over your lifetime*

WHAT DO I DO?

All of the ways I've outlined offer tax breaks to encourage you to be sensible and save money, and if you've got money spare then it's worth looking at which tax-free investment wrappers are best suited to you.

Although I am concentrating on paying off my mortgage, I have some money in the bank for easy access in case of emergency, and I have some money in an ISA, invested in the stock market (via a tracker fund), which I could do with putting more into.

I do have some money in a pension but I stopped contributing to it when I went freelance. As a self-employed person I don't have an employer to contribute on my behalf, and locking my money away for decades while I work in the precarious world of self-employment makes me nervous.

So I'm really happy about the lifetime ISA and am planning on opening one. It will allow me to save for my future and receive a government top-up but also give me access to funds in an emergency.

Even though I'd suffer the heavy penalties for taking out funds from the lifetime ISA, I think it's better, for me, to be able to get hold of the money and be charged for it than not be able to get it at all.

Of course, you have to make your own decision based on your own circumstances; think about the bonuses you receive from each savings wrapper, what you want to do with the money saved and when you'll need it.

THE NO SPEND YEAR

SKINT BUT HAPPY: GETTING THE BALANCE RIGHT

I felt the swell of nausea rise up in my stomach. I tried to stop it as I steadied myself against my bike, but before I knew it I'd vomited at the side of the road.

I felt exhausted. It was a feeling that had been building for weeks and when I got on my bicycle that afternoon I hadn't felt right, I felt worn out.

But I had to make the trip to my sister's house, thirty miles away, as we were going shopping for her wedding dress the next day. With no budget for transport my only option was to cycle it, and as much as I didn't want to get on my bike, my sister means the world to me and there was no way I was going to miss out on the day.

Even though I'd tackled far longer rides than thirty miles, today every turn of my legs felt like a gargantuan effort and, twenty miles in, a light-headed feeling came over me. It was then that I was sick.

I phoned my sister.

'Kerry, I don't feel right,' I said. 'I've just been sick.'

'What? Are you all right?' she asked.

I explained what had happened.

'Hang on,' she said. 'I'll call you back.'

A couple of minutes later, she phoned back to say her fiancé Tom was in the area on a job and he'd pick me up in his van.

When Tom turned up I loaded my bike into the back of his van and plonked myself in the front. I had to admit defeat.

The idea behind the no spend year was to live happily for free but there were points in the past twelve months where I have felt very far from happy.

The trip to my sister's house was a particularly low point and was the culmination of trying to fit too much in and pushing myself too far.

I have tried to stay positive throughout the year and committed myself to finding solutions and workarounds to obstacles. In my mind I was resolute about powering through but on the ill-fated day that I threw up my body just couldn't keep up any more.

I wanted to try to carry on mimicking my old life as closely as I could and minimise the number of things I missed out on, but in the end I had to accept that I couldn't work full-time, shuttle hundreds of miles on a bike, see my mates, spend time with my husband and organise more stuff to do the next week.

The problem with not spending money is that everything is more difficult; it involves more planning, food preparation, travel organisation and takes more time than it would otherwise do. Something has to give.

There were plenty of times that I completely screwed up the balance of my life. The most sustained of screw-ups came at the beginning of the challenge; I spent January to March working flat out because I was struggling to find ways to go out and socialise when it was cold and dark.

It was easier to bury myself in work than to try to find ways to hang out with mates when they, quite understandably, wanted to stay in the pub and eat roast dinners next to a roaring fire.

The benefit of working harder as a freelancer is that I do get paid more. However, the monetary benefit wasn't enough to compensate the loneliness and isolation I felt. I told people I was fine and adjusting to a life without consumerism but in reality I was finding it very difficult.

The more time I spent on my own without plans to see people the more I was convinced that people didn't want to see me or that I would bore them if I did see them, so it became a horrible cycle of isolation.

All this changed when spring sprang and there was better weather and more daylight. People decided they wanted to hang out again and I felt immeasurably better.

However, in turn the better weather brought something else that I really struggled with: other people's holidays.

As summer rolled around, at times I could barely contain my envy when people told me they'd booked another beach holiday or city break. There's nothing I like more than travelling abroad – except maybe cycling. Cycling abroad is top of the list.

All of a sudden people were planning exotic trips, including my own husband, who with his mates went on two holidays, one of which was a cycling holiday. Frank was doing enough by joining me on the food bit of the challenge and cycling every-where with me. He was also keen to find free ways for us to have fun and entertain ourselves, but I would never have asked him to put his life on hold because of my challenge.

Waving him off on holiday was hard though.

My eyes were green.

Envy turned to sadness when I found out my girlfriends were booking a holiday to Ibiza. For the last few years we've gone on an annual girly trip, a long weekend to a European destination.

I was gutted to miss the trip, although I was prepared for it happening. What I wasn't prepared for was my friend Trina telling me a few months before the trip that she and her fiancé Chris were planning on moving back to Australia after a decade in the UK.

The holiday to Ibiza wouldn't just be a girly jaunt, it would be a farewell-Trina trip, a last chance to spend valuable time together before she jetted off to the other side of the world. So many emotions were competing for space at the thought of missing out on time with someone who means so much to me. I was upset at her going, I was sad that I'd miss out, and I was angry with myself for embarking on something that would restrict my life so radically. And I even contemplated going, trying to convince myself that saying farewell to a friend was a legitimate reason to break the rules, but deep down I knew it wasn't justifiable.

It did bring up a lot of questions for me: why was I doing this? Why hadn't I thought about the consequences of the challenge more thoroughly? I couldn't have predicted Trina and Chris leaving, of course I couldn't, but I realised I'd relied on things staying the same during the year so that my life could carry on as close to normal as possible. It was short-sighted and selfish.

Ibiza was undoubtedly the pinnacle of my FOMO (fear of missing out) and from the pictures I saw and the stories I heard, the girls had the time of their lives. I don't begrudge them that, I just wish I could have been part of the stories.

The feeling of FOMO was undeniably present over the year, a little streak of discontentment running through my life.

It reared its ugly head when I missed out on theatre productions, gigs, weekends away and birthday celebrations. I felt it when I knew others were out having a good time without me, making memories – but they were making memories by spending money and I couldn't do that.

I'd have to find new ways to make memories with the people I cared about and celebrate milestones with them in different ways.

PARTY PEOPLE

How I celebrated people's birthdays and other special occasions was something that lots of people asked me about over the year. They were perplexed as to what I did for presents for friends and family.

We've been taught to celebrate Christmas and birthdays by exchanging bits of card and, quite often, tat that we don't need or want.

Christmas landed just a month after my challenge started, so I didn't have anything to give anyone.

I spoke to my parents, brother and sister about Christmas and asked them whether they would be happy with a present amnesty this year; I wouldn't buy anything for them and they wouldn't buy anything for me.

They were more than happy with the arrangement and agreed that swapping gifts was akin to swapping £20 notes and a bit of a pointless exercise. In fact, they got on board so readily that they extended the amnesty among themselves!

That was the adults sorted, but children are an entirely different matter and I had three nephews to think about: my sister's boys Charlie and Tommy, aged five and two, and my brother's boy Leo, also aged two.

Tommy and Leo were too young to understand the nature of presents really but Charlie, like any kid his age, was bursting with excitement at the idea of Christmas and all the new toys he would get.

I had to find a way to get all the boys a present, for free. I'm not one of those people who can make a board game out of some sticky-backed plastic and empty loo rolls; in fact I have zero talent for crafts. Luckily, when I lamented my lack of skill and imagination online, someone came to my rescue.

It was the founder of an organisation called Fab Lab London. I'd never heard of it before, despite it being bang in the middle of the City of London, a place I'm in and out of every week.

Fab Lab is based around the idea of people 'creating not consuming', which fitted perfectly with what I was trying to do with my no spend challenge, and would also help me out with gifts for the boys.

On Fridays, Fab Lab gives you access for free to every kind of creative tool and material you could possibly wish to use. It has 3D printers, laser cutters, weird tools that are used for jewellery making and so much more.

I made the boys little cars that they had to put together themselves, then attach a balloon to in order to propel them across the floor. For a personalised touch, I laser-cut their names on to the cars.

They absolutely loved them, although the boys and I did a terrible job of making them move across the floor with the balloons (but I think our shoddy building of the cars at home was to blame!).

It didn't really matter that the cars didn't propel across the floor; the boys had a lot of fun putting them together and seeing their names on them.

I did feel a bit vindicated when the boys loved the cars. They had more fun putting them together with Frank and me and trying to make them move than they would have had with anything we could have bought them.

I genuinely believe that spending time together mucking around with the cars is what the boys enjoyed, not the cars themselves.

Buoyed by this early success, I now felt less worried that others would think I was a cheapskate when it came to their birthdays. So what if I couldn't buy them something they probably didn't want anyway? I had something better to give – my time.

For Trina's birthday I arranged a bike tour around unusual places in London – secret gardens, parks and monuments. Frank, Trina, Chris and I set off from London Bridge and spent a wonderful day cycling around and I made a picnic that we ate in one of the parks.

It was a chance to celebrate Trina's birthday and to spend some quality time with her and Chris before they left to go back home and it meant so much to all of us. In addition to this, we made Trina and Chris a playlist of songs loaded on to an old USB stick that would hopefully remind them of their time in London and all of their friends.

The present didn't cost me anything except time and it was time well spent.

Similarly, I swapped my DIY skills (wa**RIGHT**
some friends to sort out the nursery for   to help
new home. I couldn't buy them a present   n their
an afternoon scraping the walls helped then
new room.   , but
                                            tiful

TIME IS NOT ON MY SIDE

While giving time instead of gifts sounds lovely, a
have a drawback – you only have a certain amoun
give. There were occasions when I stretched myse
and tried to cram too much into a short space of tir
to be there for people and ensure I didn't miss out.

Occasionally this cramming made me physically sick
the trip to my sister's, but mostly it just left me knackei

That's how I felt over the summer. Excited that the
weather meant I would be able to get out and about on my
more, I booked a ridiculous number of events in.

The biggest event was the wedding of our friends James and
Julia near Southampton, 120 miles away. Bless Frank, who agreed
to cycle with me.

Lots of our mates were going so we had someone to take our
wedding clothes down for us (at least we wouldn't look crumpled)
and as the wedding was in Julia's home town we would be camping
out in her family's back garden.

I was excited about the wedding, but the week before I came
down with a horrendous cold and lost my voice. A day in bed
meant I felt miles better, but what turned out to be a twelve-hour
bike ride was not fun – in fact, four hours of rain made it posi-
tively miserable.

We rode down on the Friday and back on the Monday, so had
two days of wedding fun and recovery, and the ride back was
miles better.

...ld have been fine in isolation but my FOMO
...ook in another trip. This time it was to Brighton,
... weekend, with six of my friends. Again Frank
with me rather than take the train.

...ght I should have sacked the trip off. It was a sixty-
...here on Saturday and then of course we promptly had
...e sixty miles back on Sunday (after staying at a friend's
...house). Of course, it's always nice to see your friends
...had only spent about an hour on the beach before
...one suggested we go for a meal and a drink (neither of
...h I could participate in).

...or the rest of the evening we sat in a pub. I could have done
...at in London. I certainly didn't need to ride 120 miles – part
...f which was over a bloody great big hill called Ditchling Beacon
in the South Downs that I nearly cried going up.

In my rush to keep on living my life and doing what my friends
were doing I hadn't taken the practical considerations into
account.

There is a happy ending to this story, even though there was
more cycling to come. The following week I had to cycle down
to see my brother and his wife, around forty miles away, so I
could meet my new niece Ivy. That was a trip that was worth
taking and I'd have cycled hundreds of miles to see her gorgeous
little face and have her squeeze my finger with her tiny hand.

A JOURNEY TOO FAR

Luckily my mum, my sister and brother and my niece and nephew
all live within a sort-of reasonable cycling distance of about forty
miles (although I appreciate that some people think I'm bonkers
and that this is not a reasonable distance at all).

However, not all of my family live close enough to cycle to;
my dad and my grandad live on the west coast of Ireland.

Usually I'd fly over to see them a few times a year and Dad comes over to the UK a few times a year too. Grandad unfortunately can't fly, so I wouldn't be able to see him for an entire year. I'd visited Ireland a couple of weeks before my challenge started and explained to him what I was doing.

When I wrote online about not seeing Grandad for a year I got a lot of stick – people who didn't know me telling me I was a bad person for not seeing my family – but Grandad was really proud of me. He has always tried to teach us the value of saving and he paid off his mortgage early too, so really I'm following in his footsteps.

It wasn't an ideal situation to be in but I knew my Grandad understood what I was doing and why I was doing it.

Bar Grandad, I've actually seen a fair bit of my family this year – probably only a jot less than I normally would – and they have been keen to come up to our house for sleepovers, which the nephews love.

We've had trips to the Science Museum and the Natural History Museum, with me cycling down and my family getting the tube, but the things I've most enjoyed have been teaching Charlie to ride a bike and the massive water fight we had in the back garden in the August heat.

The boys aren't interested in shiny new objects and other stuff; they wanted to spend time with us, playing hide and seek or making rocket ships and alien antennae out of foil.

TIME OVER STUFF

It's not just children who would prefer your time over stuff; I think we'd all prefer to spend our time with people we care about rather than accruing more things (although the throng of people on the high street each weekend may suggest otherwise).

Making crazy memories with people has been the best bit of

this year and I'd hope that my friends, on the whole, have enjoyed spending time with me even if it has been a bit restrictive on occasions.

I know some friends haven't quite got their heads around the challenge; one told me she found it hard to see me if we were just going to do free things. Another has been keen to get me drinking in the pub and always asking if I want a pint.

I've relented on occasion and let the odd person buy me a drink because it's obviously important to her, and others, that I fit in; but it actually made me feel more awkward than not drinking at all because I couldn't buy a round back. It made me feel like a piss-taker and I'd really rather have sat with my water than be badgered into accepting a paid-for drink.

Of course, I couldn't expect my friends to give up what they wanted to do for a year in order to follow me around doing free things. As I've said yes to new adventures I've had to find new people to go with.

Meeting lovely new people and making new friends has been one of the best parts of the no spend year. A lot of the new relationships I've built have been centred on getting out and about, mostly through cycling and swimming.

Previously I'd have been too nervous to try to make new friends – which is probably one of the reasons I got so stuck in a spending rut before – but in the no spend year I've had to suck it up and get out there. I always thought I was an outgoing person but now I think there was a sliver of self-consciousness under the surface that I've had to overcome.

In the first few months of the challenge I mucked up the balance of my life by staying in too much, but as the year wore on it swung the other way and the imbalance was that I was going out too much, meeting too many people and trying to fit too much in.

In the end I was forcing myself to stay in, booking time in my diary that was just for me to do absolutely nothing.

THE SIMPLE LIFE

The no spend year has been a whirlwind of activity and people and ridiculous adventures (and inadvertent cycling challenges), but through all of this I have realised that it's the simple things in life that matter.

The happiest I've been this year is when I've been out on my bike or out for a walk – things I've always enjoyed but which, in toeing the line when it comes to socialising, I had neglected before in favour of a night on the tiles.

Getting out in the fresh air and exploring new places is good for the soul and has been good for my marriage too. A long bike ride into the middle of nowhere with Frank has allowed us time to talk without the pressure of work phone calls or chores, all of which eat into our time, make us irritable and clutter our minds.

I feel I've learned more about friends and their lives, and become closer to them, just sitting in the garden with a cup of tea, having a chat.

And actually I have opened up far more. I think it would be fair to say that in the past I've been something of a closed book, preferring to let other people talk about their lives than to let people into mine, even people I'm close to. This challenge has given people a window to my life; I have laid myself bare and I think it has had a positive effect – it has brought me closer to more people and that is always a good thing.

It is not only the people I know who I want to open up to; I have been inspired by the generosity that kind-spirited strangers have shown me throughout the challenge, offering me bike parts and hair dye.

I met a wonderful family in Cheltenham who let me and Frank camp in their back garden when we attended the Cheltenham Literature Festival. The organisers of the festival put us in touch with Sally and Phil, who offered us a place to camp (with phenomenal views all the way to Bristol); and in the morning we had breakfast and a fantastic chat with them and their boys. They were incredibly generous with their home and their time and I want to be a person who has those attributes.

It costs us nothing to be kind but in our 'me me me' society we're often after our next fix, focussed on our next goal. This year has inspired me to take the blinkers off and look beyond the bigger picture and get involved in my community.

It has been small steps: working behind the makeshift bar at a friend's choir recital, volunteering to help clean up a piece of woodland in my local area and helping to paint the walls when the co-operative bike workshop, the London Bike Kitchen, opened up a second venue.

I hope to help more, especially with a local charity that aims to encourage people to cycle through free lessons and cycle rides with more confident cyclists. Getting out and about on my bike, meeting new people and helping others sounds like the perfect balance to me.

GETTING THE BALANCE RIGHT

Saving is important but you still need to have a life; these are the things I've learned that have made my life happier over the past year.

1. Embrace change

You can't expect to make a radical change to your life – like deciding to save all your money – and think that everything will just stay the same. Your life will be different; but different doesn't have to mean bad. By embracing change you may find a new hobby that you love or push yourself past limits you didn't think you ever could.

2. Prioritise

Work out what is important to you and what makes you happy and ensure you put aside time for it. Yes, you may miss out in different areas of your life but ultimately you'll be happier because you were true to the goals you wanted to achieve.

3. Simple things

I know you have a busy life – everyone does these days; that's why taking time to appreciate the small things in life is important. Whether it's the sun on your face as you walk into work or a particularly good cup of coffee, stop for a second and enjoy it – I promise it will make your day better.

4. Ignore social media

Social media is bullshit: there, I've said it. If there's one thing that will make you feel bad about yourself it's looking at the curated timeline of someone else's perfect life. It's marketing material, not their real life. They don't show you the Saturday nights they're cutting their toenails in front of *X Factor*. Don't buy into it.

5. Go outdoors

I know, I know, I'm always banging on about the outdoors. That's because getting some fresh air and a bit of Vitamin D from the sun's rays is good for you. You don't have to go far – even a brisk walk around the local park will do. It's especially good at clearing the cobwebs if you have a problem to solve.

6. Say yes

You can have an exciting life without money but you can't have an exciting life if you don't say 'yes'. Being open to new experiences and willing to have an adventure is exciting; it will take you on paths you didn't know you would travel and put you in touch with fabulous people you otherwise wouldn't have met.

7. Say no

Don't feel like you have to do things just because they're the things you've always done. If you're unhappy with your life, for whatever reason, then change that reason; you only have one life, so what's the point in doing things you don't want to do?

8. Factor in time for yourself

We all need downtime, whether it's time to read a book, give yourself a facial, or just a sit-down and a cup of tea without someone asking something of you. That has to be factored into your day and I'd suggest booking some personal time into your diary to ensure it doesn't fall by the wayside.

9. Give back

Doing something for someone else or your community will make you feel good. It doesn't have to be a big thing or even an organised event; you could make a commitment to pick up the litter on your road whenever you see it.

THE
NO
SPEND
YEAR

THE
MORBID
BIT

THE MORBID BIT

There's no easy way to say this: you're going to die and so are the people you love.

We're all going to at some point and, while it may be tempting to put your fingers in your ears and shout 'la, la, la', it's not the responsible thing to do, especially where your finances are involved. You and the people in your family need to be aware of what will happen to savings, investment and property when you, or they, die.

If you're taking control of your money then you need to think about the worst happening. We save for a rainy day, we buy insurance 'just in case' – these things may seem pessimistic but it's the practical and sensible thing to do.

I've already told you about insurance that kicks in should you kick the bucket and that's a really good place to start, especially if you own a property with another person. Frank and I have a joint life insurance policy that pays off the mortgage should one of us snuff it.

It's a good start but there's still more to do, so here's some things you need to think about:

Write a will

The best way to make sure your money goes where you want it to in the event of your death is to write a will. A will gives you the opportunity to set out in clear terms who should get your property and savings when you die.

If you die without one, which is known as dying 'intestate', then the law determines who your money goes to. For example, if you are married or in a civil partnership your half of a joint estate goes automatically to your spouse, but if you are not married or in a civil partnership, your partner is not legally entitled to anything if you die intestate.

Not only does a will make sure your money goes where you

want it to, including savings, property, jewellery and other 'chattels' (possessions), but it also makes it easier for your family to deal with your estate at a very difficult time.

Property

I'm married, so my half of our house would automatically pass to Frank if I died and vice versa, but when we first bought a property we weren't married, so we had our mortgage written under a 'joint tenants' agreement.

If you buy a property with another person there are two ways of drawing up the contract.

* **Joint tenants** (sometimes known as beneficial joint tenants): this gives you and the other person equal rights to the entire property; if you die your half goes to them automatically and you can't pass your half on through a will to someone else.

* **Tenants in common**: this allows you to own different shares of the property, so if one person puts down a bigger deposit they could claim a bigger share. Under this agreement, if you die the property doesn't automatically go to the person you bought it with – you can pass it to whoever you like.

If you're buying a home with someone else it's up to you which way you draw up the contract and it will depend entirely on your own circumstances. Note that you can switch status if your circumstances change. If you're buying with someone you want to stay with for ever then you may want to use a 'joint tenants' agreement, but if you're buying with a friend then a 'tenants in common' agreement may be better.

Pension

Of course, we all hope that we will live to a ripe old age and so need our pensions, but just in case you don't, you should think about who will receive yours.

To make sure your savings go to the person you wish them to go to, you can sign an 'expression of wish' form, which will tell the trustees of the pension (who pay out the cash) who you want to benefit.

As of April 2015, you can leave your pension – whether you've saved it personally or (more usual) through your employer – to anyone you like as either a lump sum or an income. The trustees pay out the money, not your employer, and you need to make sure you let them know who you want the beneficiary to be – your HR department should be able to help you with this. For pensions you pay into outside of work, you will need to contact your pension provider to get an expression of wish form.

Make sure you keep track of all your old pensions and that any expression of wish you change is changed for all of them, especially if your relationship status changes – for example, if you divorce and remarry you may not want your ex-spouse to benefit from your old pensions.

Savings

Like any other asset, savings can be passed on via a will or, if there's no will, they will be passed to the nearest relative via intestacy rules.

However, there are special rules around 'individual savings accounts' (ISAs) that let you inherit the ISA of your spouse or civil partner free of inheritance tax; the ISA passes from the deceased person to their living spouse or civil partner in a one-off transaction.

For example, if your wife dies with £25,000 in her ISA that she has saved up over a number of years, you will be able to inherit the ISA and keep the tax-free benefits of it (even though the annual ISA allowance is currently only £20,000).

In short . . .

Write a will. It won't take long, is worth the cost – between £150 and £300 for a joint will – and you'll be glad you've done it.

WHAT A RELIEF!

If you've stripped back your spending to the bone and are still looking to save more, then the only way to do so is by earning more.

You can brave your boss and ask for a pay rise or, if you work for yourself, spend even more time chained to your phone fielding emails at all hours. Or, you could look to the numerous tax reliefs that are available for earning a bit of cash on the side.

In a bid to keep up with the 'sharing economy' trend, the government, in its 2016 Budget, reached out to 'micro-entrepreneurs' to offer a £1,000 tax-free allowance for trading income and the same again for property income. Er . . . what?

Basically the 'trading income' means that the first £1,000 you make selling stuff on platforms like eBay is tax-free and the 'property income' means that the first £1,000 you make through renting out a room on Airbnb or renting out your driveway, for example, is also tax-free.

It also applies to those who use their hobbies and skills outside of work as a bit of a pocket-money spinner; for example, baking cakes or selling crafts. And those who hire out their own items through sharing-economy websites, whether that be their car or power tools, will also benefit.

If you earn under £1,000 doing these things there's no need to declare the income to HM Revenue & Customs, so you won't need to fill out a self-assessment tax return. If you go over either of the £1,000 thresholds (remember you get one for trading and one for property) then you have to declare the income to the taxman.

Note that you don't get £1,000 allowance for renting out a car and another £1,000 for your small cake-making sideline; it's a £1,000 total allowance for trading and £1,000 total for property.

SHARE YOUR HOME

There's an even better tax break on offer if you have a spare room to rent on a more permanent basis and are willing to take in a lodger.

Under the Rent a Room relief rules (that's a mouthful!) you can earn up to £7,500 a year from a lodger without having to declare the income to the taxman – any money made over this and you do have to.

This is a generous relief but it is only granted if the property is your main residence. It's also only granted once per property, so if you and your other half live together and you get a lodger, you still only get £7,500 of relief, not £15,000.

I've used eBay to flog a lot of stuff in the past but the Rent a Room relief has made the biggest difference to the savings I made this year. Taking in a lodger means we've taken advantage of the £7,500 of tax-free income and boosted the savings I've made during my no spend year.

We hadn't thought before about taking in a lodger, but the increased focus on paying off the mortgage brought on by the challenge made us bite the bullet and get someone in. Both Frank and I had lived in shared houses when we were younger but we had lived together, just the two of us, for around nine years and we were both concerned that having someone else around would upset the balance of our house.

We couldn't have been more wrong. Of course the extra money is nice (especially when you have a big old mortgage to pay), but having an extra person in our household has in fact been fun. As we all work full-time, and our lodger works long hours, we hardly see each other in the week and can have a nice catch-up at weekends. I'd like to think I'm quite a sociable person anyway and don't mind being around lots of people – besides, if someone needs time to themselves, they can take themselves off to their bedroom.

Of course, we didn't just get in the first person we saw, we did a round of interviews and met a few different people until we found the person we got on best with. If you are nervous about renting a room out don't be afraid to ask them for references from work, to ensure they can pay the rent, or even from colleagues and friends.

We didn't do any of this, preferring to rely on gut feeling and it has worked out well for us.

I would definitely recommend it if you get a lovely lodger like we have, and it has the added bonus of making me a lot tidier as I'm no longer inclined to leave dirty washing all over the place!

THE
NO
SPEND
YEAR

THE NO SPEND
ENDS – OR
DOES IT?

As the weeks ticked down to 26 November 2016 and the end of the no spend challenge, there were two questions people kept asking me.

'What are you going to buy first?'

'Are you going to have a big splurge?'

I think this says a lot about how we've been trained to consume. People were fixated on what I was going to acquire, rather than what I had acquired, which was a huge amount of savings and lots of experience and knowledge.

I hadn't bought anything in a year; surely (the thinking went) I would want to make my offering to the shopping gods now?

The truth is, there is no big pot of money to splurge or offer up to the shopping gods. The aim of this challenge wasn't just to jump out of the consumer cycle – although that's an important part – mainly, I had the serious financial goal of overpaying my mortgage.

As well as my standard (hefty) mortgage payment going out each month – the one I have to pay so I don't lose my home – I also paid extra amounts towards my mortgage over the course of the year.

The reason for doing this is twofold: by taking chunks out of the balance of the mortgage you cut down the amount of time you spend paying it (in my case I have a 25-year mortgage) because you are paying the balance (or capital) back more quickly.

This has the knock-on effect of cutting the amount of interest you pay over the term of the mortgage. Overpaying means you pay back your home loan quicker and you pay less interest to the bank – win-win.

As I've been overpaying the mortgage over the year I don't actually have a huge pot of money that I could blow, even if I wanted to.

I suppose you want to know how much I overpaid?

Drum roll, please!

When I started the challenge in November 2015, my mortgage stood at just over £230,000. Over the past twelve months, by cutting spending to essentials only, taking in a lodger and making use of a £7,500 tax break, and channelling spare money into the mortgage, I have overpaid:

£22,493.

That's a shade under 10% of my mortgage and I am delighted with the result. Factoring in the regular payments that I have to make anyway, the money now owed on our house is a massive step closer to being sub-£200,000, which feels like a real milestone.

As I set out at the beginning of the book, I did have to pay my bills. In case you've forgotten, here's a run-down of the bills I continued to pay:

Mortgage
Money to charity
Council tax
Gas and electricity
Phone bills
Water services
House and contents insurance
Life insurance

Money to help family
Critical illness insurance
Washing machine insurance
TV licence
Internet
Bank account fee

The monthly total of the household bills is £1,896.76, so my half equals £948.38, or £11,380.56 for the year.

On top of this I had to buy groceries: food, toiletries and cleaning products. If you remember, this is where my husband joined in with the challenge and over the course of the year we jointly spent £1,644.97, which means our average weekly grocery shop cost us just £31.63.

If you'd like a bit more of a breakdown then you're in luck. Throughout the year I have created the world's most boring spreadsheet that details every item I bought at the supermarket. Every last banana, loaf of bread and bottle of washing up liquid is accounted for. Rock 'n' roll.

The total spend for the year I've already told you was £1644.97 for the both of us.

Of this spending, £100.91 was non-edibles. This accounts for things like toiletries, washing up liquid, clothes washing powder, foil, tampons, kitchen roll, bin liners etc; anything you can't eat.

That means we spent £1544.06 on food over the course of the year. Worked out roughly, that money had to cover three meals a day each of us for seven days a week for 52 weeks which totals 2184 meals. I say roughly because we also had snacks, Frank went on a holiday a couple of times so wasn't around for a week or two, we ate at friend's and family's houses sometimes, and I also have to attend work events now and again where I am fed.

This meant our 2184 meals cost us the equivalent of 70p each. Not bad going.

My wondrously dull spreadsheet also tells me just how many

of each item we purchased throughout the year, and I can tell you we like bananas. A lot.

This is a list of the top 20 items we purchased over the course of the year in quantity and total cost (I know, I'm a loser!):

1. Bananas: 363 bananas at £58.49
2. Tins of tomatoes: 295 tins at £88.55
3. Soya milk: 164 cartons at £137.75
4. Peppers: 123 peppers at £34.05
5. Chickpeas: 115 tins at £38.67
6. Baked beans: 90 tins at £24.13
7. Oats: 67 packs at £26.35
8. Houmous: 63 tubs at £43.29
9. Tofu: 63 packs at £81.25
10. Spring onions: 47 bunches at £20.29
11. Onions: 46 packs at £35.02
12. Bread: 46 loaves at £44.98
13. Spinach: 45 bags at £42.75
14. Potatoes: 44 2.5kg bags at £56.88
15. Pasta: 38 packs at £11.58
16. Frozen berries: 36 packs at £59.80
17. Fresh tomatoes: 31 packs at £14.61
18. Beetroot: 23 packs at £18.97
19. Lentils: 23 packs at £24.50
20. Rice: 21 packs at £17.82

Rice, lentils, chickpeas, potatoes and tinned tomatoes with veg made up the majority of our meals, with a bit of fruit thrown in so we didn't get scurvy.

Lots of people told me that if I really wanted to cut down to essentials then I should be living on £1 a day for food but that wouldn't have been realistic considering the amount of exercise I do, and neither would it have made me happy. The challenge was to try and live my life happily but spending as little as possible and most people said a realistic grocery budget was £30 for one person – we've gone just over that and covered two (very active) people.

I'm happy with my achievement when it comes to grocery spending. If you compare it to the £2,850 we spent in the previous year, we've cut the grocery bill by 42%. I'm putting that in the 'win' column.

Adding up my half of the bills, plus the total spend on groceries, it comes to £13,025.53 for the entire year.

That means for every £1 I spent, I overpaid £1.70.

Additional spending

So did I spend any money that wasn't 'permitted'? I'll tell you the scenarios and let you judge for yourselves.

The first instance was when my next-door neighbour told me he'd had some bits fixed on his roof and had given the roofer the OK to fix a missing tile between our house and his (we live in a terrace); the work had already been done and the roofer had already been paid. The repair cost £100 and we owed the neighbour £50. I handed over the money because it did need doing (I just hadn't realised), and my neighbour didn't know I was on a no spend year. As far as I'm concerned, that spend ws unavoidable.

The second instance occurred on holiday when I spent £1.95 on chips at the seaside the day that all I could find to eat in the local shop was pork pies. They were possibly the best chips I've ever eaten! We can argue about whether I should have bought them or not, but I needed to eat and I'm pretty happy that £1.95 is the total I've spent on takeaway hot food other than things I've made myself with pre-bought groceries.

POVERTY VERSUS FRUGALITY

There were lots of questions and some criticism about the bills I was paying during my no spend year. Some people felt I shouldn't be paying any at all, but that wasn't realistic or sensible.

Others criticised me for continuing to pay for my telephone and broadband, but as I work as a freelance journalist, if I don't have these things I can't work. Without the ability to work, I would have had no money and wouldn't have been able to pay my bills and keep the roof over my head.

The third bill that raised eyebrows was the TV licence. Arguably I could have cut it out and ditched the TV, but Frank was having none of that (he wasn't giving up telly as well as having to support me on my challenge!). And in fairness, I use the BBC for more than just TV – radio and news too – so for £12.12 a month I think it's bloody good value and well worth supporting.

Further criticism came from people who weren't worried about the details of the bills but thought what I was doing was insulting to those living in poverty.

I think this is where people misconstrued the no spend year. This wasn't a challenge to live in poverty; it was a personal challenge to live as frugally as I possibly could. It was a challenge to see whether I could extricate myself from the social norms of purchasing, whether that be clothes, gig tickets or meals out, and cut back as far as I could.

There is a huge difference between poverty and frugality; poverty is not a choice, but frugality is.

I could still pay my bills and had the means to do so. I could also buy food and made the choice to keep my food bills as low as possible. All along, the decision to spend as little as possible was my choice, not something forced upon me by circumstance.

I wanted to be as frugal as possible in order to hit a financial goal and to prove to myself that I didn't need to be part of the consumer rat race.

The no spend year was not about taking poverty and turning it into a lifestyle – I don't think anyone would ever choose to live in poverty – it was about seeing what I needed to be happy and freeing myself from the clutches of consumerism.

BEING FREE

Freedom is something I've thought a lot about over the past year. You may think that 'being free' is anathema to this challenge – surely by restricting myself so much, I couldn't possibly be free in any way?

I actually think the reverse is true. For me freedom comes in two forms, but essentially they are two sides of the same coin.

Let me explain.

In overpaying my mortgage I am getting closer to being mortgage-free far earlier than the twenty-five years the bank has me signed up to. If I stuck to the bank's plan for my debt I would be fifty-six by the time I had paid off my mortgage.

If I carry on as I am now, I will have it paid off in less than a decade. That sounds much better to me. Without a mortgage to pay I would have a large amount of financial independence.

Like most people, my mortgage is my largest outgoing and if I no longer had to pay it, and just had to find money for my other bills, I would be able to work less and spend more time on my hobbies and doing the things I really love.

Even if you haven't got a mortgage but you do have debts, such as loans or overdrafts, the principle of financial freedom can still be applied. The quicker you pay off your loans – rather than paying them at the amount set by the lender – then the sooner you will have spare money to save or to channel into something you love.

Being unencumbered by debt gives you choice; it gives you more financial freedom to do as you please with your hard-earned cash.

You can measure financial freedom in the pounds you save and the money you no longer have to pay to the bank; but there's another freedom that is more intangible.

Over the past year I feel that I've broken free from consumerism. Not being able to spend means there's no need for me to go to my local shopping centre, I have no reason to build Amazon wish lists, or browse online for hours.

I'm no longer bogged down by the tyranny of choice that rules over us in our consumer world, I'm taking no notice of the adverts that constantly entice us to spend, and I feel absolutely no desire to keep up with the Joneses, the Kardashians or anyone else.

When you give yourself a budget of zero, you don't give a shit about spending any more.

Not only is it a great feeling, not being beholden to a society that places consumerism and possession above all else, but also, all that time I used to spend buying things I now have free to spend doing things I actually care about, things that enrich my life in a way that purchasing never ever could.

I've come to realise that we've all been sold the corporate lie that we can buy our way to happiness and that we should chain ourselves to desks for eight hours a day in order to make money to buy that happiness. Well, I call bullshit on that. I refuse to buy into that lie any more. I don't want to spend my life working in order to fuel the corporate machine; I don't want to be working to line the pockets of the banks or big businesses on the high street.

Financial freedom and freedom from consumerism are intertwined. The less I buy the more I have to save and the closer I get to financial freedom. I understood this principle – buy less and you'll have more money to save – even before my no spend year, but in an abstract way. The last year has turbocharged that idea and made me actually realise just how little I need to make me happy.

SAVINGS ASSESSMENT

From a sensible financial-planning point of view, my idea of financial freedom has also been re-evaluated. My only financial goal has been to pay off my mortgage; mortgages are the biggest debt most of us will ever have and I hate the idea of being beholden to the bank – especially for decades of my working life. Getting rid of debt before saving makes sense to me. If you had £1,000 in savings and £500 on your overdraft, you'd be daft not to pay off the overdraft that's costing you money.

However, from talking to numerous people about money over the past year and discussing my plan with them, I've realised I also need to start thinking about long-term saving and retirement. That's a scary prospect and one I don't actually want to think about, partly because I think I'll never actually properly retire in the way my grandparents did.

Those of us now in our twenties, thirties and forties are going to live and work for much longer than older generations – a retirement age of sixty-five just isn't realistic any more. Most of us are also saving far too little to fund a decent retirement (I definitely fall into this camp).

It would be nice to have the option of retirement though, so I am going to start putting something aside for my old age, not just throwing all my spare cash at the mortgage. I've promised myself that when the new Lifetime ISAs are introduced in April I'll open one.

They're perfect for me because I'm self-employed and don't receive an employer contribution into a pension (if I did I'd be paying into a workplace pension). Instead, I can save up to £4,000 into a Lifetime ISA each year, invest the money (it would be insane to leave it in cash where its value would be eroded), and I'll get a 25% top-up from the government for doing so.

The catch is that I can't take the money out before I reach sixty without a 5% penalty and the loss of the government top-up, but the benefit is that I can access the savings so if my freelance work dries up totally I will have an extra pot of emergency money to fall back on.

If I want to retire, it's up to me to make provision for that. And it's up to you to take control of your finances too.

We are living in a far less paternalistic world than even a few decades ago, and no one else is going to check that we've saved enough for our retirements. The government will ensure that you are auto-enrolled into a workplace pension (although you can opt out), but it is up to you to save more and ensure you save enough to avoid an old age spent either in poverty or working until you drop.

I know that you know saving money is a good idea – we all know that – but I also know it's hard to do, and that sometimes it doesn't feel worth it.

Over the past year, my challenge, and my openness about my plans to save, have given people a green light to talk to me about their own money. In hushed tones people have talked to me about the most British of taboos: how much money they earn and, crucially, how much money they spend.

It has been an eye-opening experience and has confirmed to me that we all know we should be squirrelling away more but the cost of modern life is high and people don't want to miss out.

If you are worried that you're not saving enough or you're spending too much, and I'll assume you are as you're reading this book, then take heart from the fact that you are not alone. Ironically, a lot of people who are concerned about spending too much continue to spend just to keep up with people – but those people are probably just as concerned about spending too much!

It's a vicious circle and one that could easily be challenged by someone piping up and saying: 'Shall we knock the cocktail bar on the head tonight and do something free?'

Some of my own friends, people who I had always thought didn't worry about money because they seemed to spend with abandon have said to me on the quiet that they need to rein in their spending.

Other people I know, and people online who I don't know, have joined in with the challenge, some for a set period of time and some taking on certain elements of it.

A work friend, Mark, has started his own challenge to see how many days he can get from payday before he has to spend any money. I really like this idea as I think it's more realistic than stopping yourself spending entirely. Mark has a young family and knows he will never be able to stop spending outright, but holding out on spending for as long as you can after payday is a clever way to ensure your money stretches more comfortably until the next payday.

Other people have committed to not buying certain items, such as gadgets, clothes and books, for a certain period of time (normally a month). And some have vowed to use up the make-up and toiletries they have before buying more.

That's the thing about a no spend challenge – you can personalise it to fit your spending habits. We all have our own spending vices that we know we need to curb, so it makes sense to make up a challenge to suit your own.

MORE THAN MONEY

When I started the challenge, I'll admit my focus was on saving money and paying off my mortgage, I hadn't thought about the impact it would have on me personally. I wouldn't have been able to predict that the past twelve months would not only revitalise my finances but totally change me as a person.

And I think the changes have been for the better.

The challenge has pushed me beyond my own self-enforced limits and forced me to open up to new experiences and to new people. I'm happy saying 'yes' to activities that I may have shied away from before because I'm less worried about failing and less concerned about what people think.

I have become far more adventurous and confident in my own abilities. Even small things like learning how to look after my bike have made me more self-reliant.

My self-reliance has practical benefits but it has also increased my confidence when it comes to my peers. I'm less concerned that I'm missing out or that I don't fit in – I haven't 'fitted in' for the past year and it's been fine; nothing bad happened. I chose to live a different life and I didn't automatically lose all my friends and live like a hermit – in fact I have gained friends and an armful of experiences I would not have had otherwise.

I'd like to think that my new-found sense of adventure has rubbed off on others too. They have been kind enough to go along with me in my challenge and I don't think hanging out with me has been a terrible hardship for them (at least I hope it hasn't!). They have embraced scenarios that they wouldn't have otherwise and I'd like to think that we can all carry on with our adventures even now the year is over.

We live in a world that bombards us with choices and I have opted out of making the choices of which restaurant to eat in, what smartphone to buy, what book to read first, what clothes are trendy . . . Too much choice is exhausting and it actually has a name: decision fatigue.

This happens when you are fed up with making choices, and it explains why Facebook's Mark Zuckerburg owns a wardrobe of identical grey T-shirts – it's so he doesn't have to waste time and energy deciding what to wear.

The lack of choice I've had was liberating. I've swapped wasting time on lots of small decisions that in the big scheme of life don't really matter for making decisions about the best way to spend all the time I have freed up by jumping out of consumerism.

I'm not pretending that everything over the past year has been a bed of roses. There were people who were not willing to be part of the challenge and couldn't understand why I was doing it. Fair enough.

And of course I have missed out on some special occasions, holidays and fun events. But bar hangovers and sunshine, did I really miss out that much? Maybe I would have been invited out and away more if I hadn't been on a no spend year, but that doesn't mean I sat indoors all year worrying about what my mates were up to.

The one thing I definitely didn't expect was to do more with no money than I did when I had money to spend. On balance I think I have made huge gains in my life.

So what happens now that I can spend again? In truth I'm a little nervous about having the option back! Life was simpler when I had less choice. At first the military organisation required for my food and travel was a complete pain, but now it's become my norm and I can't see myself dropping the meal planning, weekly trips to the supermarket with my list, or the cycling.

Now every last penny doesn't have to go to the mortgage I can dust off the cobwebs from my purse; but it will be a surreal experience to have disposable income again. The first thing I bought was a huge round of drinks for my friends and family and all the people who have supported me over the past year.

The second thing I bought was a plane ticket to Ireland to celebrate my grandad's ninetieth birthday the weekend after the challenge finished. I also plan to visit my friend Lauren in Canada; I haven't seen her in three years but she has been amazingly supportive over the past twelve months and I need to give her a big squeeze.

There are items that desperately need replacing. Because I didn't stockpile loads of items or buy a tonne of new clothes before the challenge, everything I own is at least a year old if not far older, and much of it is on its last legs now.

Realistically I need some new jeans as all mine have bike-saddle marks on the bum, some new T-shirts to replace the ones ingrained with body odour, a new coat as I've managed to get a tear in mine, and some new boots and trainers – the ones I own have worn through. The obscene cycling leggings will have to go too!

Oh, and some moisturiser. Definitely some moisturiser.

I'll also have to spend some money on some practical things like servicing my bicycle and getting some new tyres to ensure it is roadworthy and safe. After 6,500 miles plus, bald tyres are a given.

On a more practical note I'll go to the dentist, especially as I chipped a part of a filling back in April.

In answer to the question of whether I'm going to splurge loads of money, I'd have to say it's a resounding 'no'. I want to replace the things I actually need rather than run riot on Oxford Street splashing the cash for the sake of it.

And I know what I need. And it's not a lot. A few T-shirts and pairs of jeans and a couple of pairs of shoes have seen me through this last year, so why would I need any more now?

I want to ensure the items I do buy are good quality though, so I don't have to replace them again any time soon, rather than buying loads of cheap items that I don't need and that are likely to fall apart in a short space of time.

I said at the beginning that our minimalist leanings had encouraged us to throw out around 80% of our belongings but in truth I think we could have thrown out far more.

There's no way that I will once again take a place at the starting blocks in the consumer rat race. It would be such a waste of twelve months of learning and growing to go back to my bad habits of frittering money on useless items, the same old activities, and on things that don't make me happy.

Now I have got food shopping, meal planning and batch cooking down to a fine art, why would I go back to buying £3 meal deals? I won't.

Now I know how many free activities are up for grabs every week, why would I default to just spending money? I won't.

Now I know being outdoors on my bike, meeting like-minded people and achieving something, makes me tick, why would I swap it for endless nights in the pub? I won't.

You see, my whole mindset has shifted. We are often told who to be by being sold a life but over the past year I didn't have money to buy that life anymore. I suppose what I'm trying to say is that by striping everything back I was forced to look at who I really was. Instead of just going with the flow, I was confronted by myself and by questions about what I really wanted to do with my life.

I believe a lot of us do stuff just to fill time, to fit in, to stop our boredom, or because we're told to do it by society. I know I have been guilty of filling gaps in my life with buying and reaching for the 'next thing' rather than thinking about what it is I really want. If I'd bothered to have asked myself that when spending, I doubt I'd have answered that the thing I really wanted was a designer lamp or new pair of shoes.

It's scary to think about what you really want from your life and nerve-wracking to try and implement changes, especially if you don't know whether they're going to pay off. Being scared by something you want to do is better than feeling comfortable in a life you never really signed up to.

Before I was happy to follow an easier path, one that was well-trodden: get job, buy house, work, work, work, retire.

Now I'm questioning why it has to be like that. I want to live a life that doesn't follow these rules, that isn't dictated to me by convention. I want to be scared.

Having looked at my life from the outside, I can say without a shadow of a doubt that I'm far happier now.

I lived happily for free for twelve months and I can continue to live happily for less from now on too, albeit with a few pints and some holidays thrown in! The life I've built over the past year has been eye-opening, exciting and adventure-filled; why would I want to change that?

I know now, beyond all doubt, that the best things in life aren't *things* at all.

THE
NO
SPEND
YEAR

QUIZ: WHAT SORT OF SHOPPER ARE YOU?

1. How often do you check your balance when you take cash out?
   a) Every time I take money out
   b) When it gets nearer payday
   c) Er . . . never

2. Do you know how much you spent on groceries last month?
   a) Down to the last baked bean
   b) I have a rough idea
   c) Ask Waitrose

3. Which of these phrases sums up your attitude to money?
   a) A penny saved is a penny earned
   b) You can't take it with you
   c) Champagne lifestyle, lemonade pockets

4. You have a fancy work do to attend. You:
   a) Reuse an outfit you have
   b) Buy something new but inexpensive
   c) Spend a fortune on a new outfit – you want to make an
      impression

5. It's lunchtime at work. You:
   a) Pull out your home-made sandwiches wrapped in foil
   b) Buy a £3 meal deal
   c) Treat yourself to lunch at Pret with a latte to take out

6. How do you pay for your purchases?
   a) Cash or direct debit, only spending the money you have
   b) Credit card but you pay the balance off in full
   c) Credit cards and store cards, paying off the minimum amount each month

7. You're going to a birthday party. You:
   a) Spend time making a home-made gift
   b) Research online and buy a gift a week in advance
   c) Panic and overspend on a present on the day of the party

8. The sales are on in the shops. You:
   a) Stay at home, I hate shopping
   b) Brave the shops but with a budget in mind
   c) Call a taxi in advance to transport your bags home

Mostly A: Sensible saver
Do you really need this book?! You know your way around a budget and are careful with your money.

Planning, using what you have and only spending when absolutely necessary, is your style and that's to be commended.

Just make sure you give yourself wiggle room in the budget for a little treat now and again to reward yourself for your thriftyness. You still need to have a life.

Mostly B: Savvy spender
You've got a pretty good handle on your financial situation. You know how much money you have to spend and usually stick to your budget, with the occasional blow-out.

Although you're not out every weekend splashing the cash on champagne or buying designer clothes, you probably find you fritter away money on the smaller purchases like lunches and coffees.

Have a look at your spending to identify where money is leaking out of your bank account – all those small spends can really add up.

Mostly C: Super-splurger

Wow, you love to spend money! Shopping may be your main hobby and you're good at it. But you need to think about the future, not just the here and now. This is especially true if you're using credit cards to make your purchases and racking up lots of debt.

If you have debt, you need to concentrate on paying it off; and if you don't, put your money to better use by setting up a direct debit to transfer some money into a savings account every payday – then you can shop guilt-free with the money left.

WHAT CAN I DO?

You may be wondering how my, rather extreme, challenge can possibly be applicable to you. Well it can:

1. Think about the areas where you know you waste money or where you spend too much. If you're being honest with yourself, you probably know what you fritter money on.
2. Check your bank statements. You don't need to look at a whole year's worth, a couple of months will be good enough. This will help you pinpoint other areas where money is vanishing out of your account.
3. Keep a spending diary for a week. Jot down your purchases, right down to magazines and money you put in the parking meter. It could also be helpful to note how you feel when you spend; are you bored, tired, happy?
4. By now you should have a good idea of where your money is going. Ask yourself whether the things you are buying are making you happy. Identify why you spend money, maybe when you're sad or bored or stressed. And most importantly, what can you cut out?
5. Now think about something that you'd love to do. Maybe you want to travel the world, take a year out to write a book,

retrain for another job, or learn to drive and afford to buy a car.

6. OK, so this is the maths bit. Work out, even a rough estimate, of how much you'd need to save in order to achieve your long-term goal.

7. Once you know how much you need to save break it down into smaller monthly saving goals that are achievable (this is key – you'll be quickly disheartened if you set yourself unachievable goals).

8. Weigh up what you want. Do you want to spend money on things that might make you happy in the short term or do you want to save for something that matters to you in the long term?

9. Try a mini no spend challenge. Whether it's a week-long ban or deciding to stop spending on a particular thing for a month. See how much money you save and whether your life really is worse because you're not spending £3 a day on a coffee (I bet it's not!).

10. It's an oldie but a goodie: draw up a budget. Now you know what you can live without then you can plan your spending – factoring in a couple of treats, otherwise you'll fall off the wagon pretty quickly.

Hopefully these 10 steps will help you think about your money and take control of it. It will help you identify what you fritter money on and why you spend money. If you these things then you are better able to avoid situations in which you spend needlessly.

This isn't about wagging a figure at you and telling you to spend less and save more, you know you should be doing that. This is about weighing up short term gains against longer term goals and deciding what will really make you happy.

I bet that achieving a long-term goal will make you far happier than anything you can buy in the shops.

WHAT HAPPENED NEXT . . .

I couldn't have predicted the impact of the No Spend Year on my life.

I knew my parsimony would save me a lot of money. I knew my mortgage would be significantly lower after the twelve months ended. And I knew that I would feel proud that I had pushed myself out of my comfort zone.

But the impact of those 366 days (it was a leap year, remember!) has been far more wide-reaching than on my bank account alone.

It changed me in more ways than I expected or thought possible. But let me tell you about that in a bit, because I'm sure you want to know the answer to the question I get asked constantly: did I go back to my old ways?

In a word: no.

A lot of people were expecting me to go crazy at the end of the year, hitting Oxford Street with my credit card, indulging in a shopping frenzy. But it didn't happen.

There were, of course, things I had to replace. My clothes were tatty and ripped, and in truth my T-shirts didn't smell great. Shoes had holes in and so did my coat. I knew I'd have to replace them but I didn't realise how stressful doing so would be.

Every purchase I made was tinged with feelings of guilt, even though I was replacing basic clothing items that I needed. Handing over my card in a shop felt alien and I can't say I enjoyed the experience.

I spent a long time working out what I needed to buy, asking myself the ever-present question: do I need it or do I just want it?

If I established that I needed something, then I researched the best value and quality. People assumed I would buy either the cheapest items, in keeping with my low-spend policy, or blow loads of cash on expensive items, but I fell somewhere in the middle.

Instead of buying cheap jeans, I bought branded ones because I know they'll last. I'm not interested in the brand; I just don't want to have to go shopping again because my cheap jeans have already worn through.

I've established that shopping is my least favourite way to spend my free time. And it may sound a bit bah-humbug, but I don't enjoy shopping for others either.

During the No Spend Year I couldn't buy people birthday or Christmas presents. This is a part of the challenge that people ask me about often; while they might be thinking of curbing their spending on themselves, they can't get their heads round stepping back from swapping Christmas presents or marking a birthday with a beautifully wrapped gift. Consumerism has a tight grip when it comes to gift giving, and we've been conditioned to think that purchasing an item (that the person probably doesn't really want anyway) is the best way to show our love.

The present amnesty in my family has lasted, long after my challenge ended. I no longer buy any presents for the adults in my family, and they don't buy any for me. Christmas and birthdays pass without the exchanging of gift bags; we spend time together instead.

Admittedly it's not a concept you can explain to six-year-olds! I'm not such a terrible auntie that I don't buy my nephews and niece birthday presents but the types of gifts I give are different. Before I would have bought a piece of plastic crap from the Argos catalogue that would have ended up marooned under a bed.

Not now. As the children are getting older, it's much more fun to gift them an experience. It might be a birthday picnic in the park or a trip to the theatre; whatever it is, it's something they remember, a lovely memory of time you spent with them. That is much more important than a toy they will play with for a day and then forget about.

The irony is, of course, that often experiences can cost more than a toy, but that's money I don't mind spending. You can't put a price on spending quality time with the people you love.

That's not to say I'm frivolous. It would be almost impossible for me to go back to how I was after ingraining new habits so deeply.

I still cycle almost everywhere, and have actually covered even more miles than during the challenge. Although if I get an invite for a wedding 120 miles away, I'll get the train this time!

I'm still regimented about the food shop and keeping our shopping bill low. We still only spend around £35 a week on our grocery shop and throw the odd bottle of wine in now and again.

I've been out for dinners and to the pub, but compared to how I was pre-challenge, I spend nowhere near as much time or money sipping pints. I won't lie, it's nice to be able to meet a friend for a quick catch-up over a glass of wine rather than trying to arrange a trip to a museum or art gallery in deepest darkest winter. But I've realised just how much I like to be outdoors – a bit like a dog, I'm happiest when I'm in the fresh air!

Which is probably why I've started to take my cycling a bit more seriously. I've been spending a lot of time outdoors riding increasingly long distances, pushing myself to go further.

One thing a year of not spending taught me is that I'm pretty stubborn and I like to challenge myself, and riding for hours, overnight and over hundreds of miles is certainly a challenge. I've even had another wild camping and cycling holiday in the Scottish Highlands, although the weather wasn't quite as amazing as the holiday during the challenge! Rain lashed down, wind threatened to run us off the road and we were bloody knackered, but in an odd way it was still fun (particularly as we had the luxury of getting the train when conditions got too difficult and dangerous to ride in).

I didn't quite expect cycling to become such a huge part of my life. When I started the no spend year, I knew I'd have to spend a lot of hours in the saddle getting from A to B, to events, nights out and even to a wedding.

However, it gave me so much more than that. It opened me up to a community of people who I now consider good friends, people who may have come into my life because of cycling but aren't just part of it because we both like bikes.

I'm grateful for those new friendships, and the existing ones, the people who helped me through the year, who went out of their way to be accommodating.

In fact, I'm grateful for everything. By being unable to put your hand in your pocket to get you out of a jam, you do start to appreciate all the things you take for granted. The fact that I am healthy and didn't need to purchase prescriptions; that I was physically capable of riding my bike all year, were things that I would have taken for granted previously, but not now.

I appreciate all the small joys in life far more and have realised there are far more important things than work.

In the years before the no spend year I was caught up in the idea that my career and work were the most important things. That my value was correlated by my title, my salary and how hard I worked. And I worked hard, I competed in the competitive games of 'I'm so busy' and 'I'm so stressed', because I thought if I didn't people would assume I was lazy and unambitious – and when you're looking for career prestige they're the last things you want people to think about you!

Well, forget that. Since the year ended I have worked less. I'm not embarrassed to say I want to scale back work, that I'm not happy pushing harder for more money and more kudos. I know I don't need as much money to live on, so I don't need to work as hard.

Now on a Friday I go for a bike ride or do a surprise school pick-up with my nephew. And it's great. I have less money but I'm happier and hopefully by riding with a friend and seeing my nephew, I'm making other people happy too.

Part of it is having the confidence to let go of the fear of what people will think about me. I used to be constrained by the idea that I should do what people expected of me, what was right and what was normal. It's how I ended up with loads of social-status consumer goods, a too-big house and burnout from work in the first place.

Now the opinions of people who don't know me don't matter. Those who do know and love me don't care how many hours I work or how many things I own; they just want me to be happy.

And because I've realised this I'm less scared of failing. I'm more willing to take risks and find out what makes me happy, even if it doesn't fit in with everyone else's idea of where I should be.

I wasn't exaggerating when I said the year changed my life. It has had a profound effect on how I see myself and others, and what I want from my life. I'm not pretending I know all the answers but I'm certainly more open to what they may be.

Let's talk money

You didn't think I'd let you go without talking a bit about money, did you? You don't get off that easily.

During the challenge I was astounded by how open people were with me about their own financial situations. They told me their spending vices, the figures they'd racked up on credit cards and the hopes they had not only for their financial situation but for their life.

And I'm glad to say that hasn't stopped. People still divulge their money secrets and ask me for advice.

I'd like to think that I've had some part in making money a less taboo subject. I know some people thought it was vulgar for me to talk about what I'd saved but I think it's important we have candid conversations about cash.

As I sit here and reflect on the past year, the UK's unsecured debt pile stands at £200 billion. That's right, £200 billion, that people have racked up on credit cards, overdrafts and car loans (a huge and worrying problem we're saving up for the not-so-distant future).

We're hitting debt levels not seen since the 2007–8 financial crisis. Just a decade on and we've forgotten the lessons we should have learned when unsustainable mortgage debt made everything go 'bang'.

I hate to be a doom-monger, but we're sitting on the cusp of another debt crisis. Our debt levels are huge and the Bank of England has just increased interest rates for the first time in a decade. While a move from 0.25% to 0.5% may not seem like a lot, it's the symbolic gesture that we need to take heed of; it means that the Bank thinks the economy and all of us can now handle higher rates and they will keep going up (albeit slowly), having an impact on the cost of the debt we have.

Oh, and let's not forget inflation is soaring, meaning everything is getting more expensive but wages aren't rising in line to cover the extra cost.

Too much debt, higher interest rates, higher cost of living and stagnant wages. You don't need to be a financial whizz to understand that that's a dangerous combination.

What can you do about it? As ever, it comes back down to sensible financial planning, budgeting, watching what you spend and living within your means.

Just know that you have control over your money and where it goes, and only you can make the decision about whether the things you're buying are truly making you happy. If you've read this book then I hope you have a better idea of how to handle your cash, and if you do take back control I can promise you you'll feel much happier.

And I should know, I'm not just a tight-arse, I'm a professional tight-arse now!

ACKNOWLEDGEMENTS

Where do I start with the thank-yous, there are so many.

It has to be with Anna Bowes who gave me the confidence, over a boozy work lunch, to pitch the idea as an article and to Hilary Osborne at the Guardian for giving me space to blog about it.

This book wouldn't have been possible without my agent Lauren who been my biggest cheerleader. You backed me from the start and made me believe I could be an author. The same goes for my editor Charlotte who has held my hand, provided pointers and encouragement when I've most needed it, and Vero, my publicist, who is unrelentingly positive.

All my love to my family who have schlepped to visit me when I couldn't visit them: Mum, Dad, Pam, Danny, Millie, Kerry, Tom, and to my nephews Charlie, Tommy, and Leo and little niece Ivy (thanks for the impromptu sleepovers, kids, they made my year). And my Grandad, who I couldn't see this year. I've missed you.

To all my friends, who have put up with my cooking and cooked for me in return. Who have been dragged to free events and accommodated my odd requests: Rowan, Leon, Katie, Simon, Trina, Chris, Colette, Cat, Emmylou, Dan, Laura, Henry, David,

Jo, Matt, James, Julia, Luke, Alasdair, Jess, Christine, Dawn, Ronke, Lucy, Emma, Paul, Lou, and Vaughan. And Lauren, who supported me across the pond from Canada – I wish you could have been here.

And thank you to people who have shown me such kindness even though they didn't need to: Michelle who sent hair dye, Bean who sent brake pads, Jenni who helped with my bike, Caroline and Lee who sent beauty supplies, Amber who donated a shopping trolley and Sally, Phil and their boys who showed us such hospitality in Cheltenham. And all the other people out there in the Twitterverse who have given me tips and encouragement – thank you, you kept me going.

The biggest thank you is reserved for my husband. Without you the challenge wouldn't have happened. This book shows just how far we've come, and not just on our bikes. This book is for you.

An invitation from the publisher

Join us at www.hodder.co.uk, or follow us
on Twitter @hodderbooks to be a part of
our community of people who love the very
best in books and reading.

Whether you want to discover more about a book
or an author, watch trailers and interviews, have the
chance to win early limited editions, or simply browse
our expert readers' selection of the very best books,
we think you'll find what you're looking for.

And if you don't, that's the place to tell us what's missing.

We love what we do, and we'd love you to be a part of it.

www.hodder.co.uk

@hodderbooks

HodderBooks

HodderBooks